Searching for Intimacy in Marriage

THE ROLE THAT EMOTION PLAYS IN CREATING UNDERSTANDING AND CONNECTEDNESS IN MARRIAGE

Bryan Craig

Editing and page composition by Ken McFarland

Note: Because the subject matter of this book necessarily focuses on couples and
the two partners a couple includes, grammatical rules concerning agreement in
"number" (singular/plural) are not always strictly followed, in order to avoid the
awkward repetition of such terms as "his or her," and "he and she."

The author assumes full responsibility for the accuracy of all facts, statistics, and
quotations as cited in this book.

ISBN: 1-57847-035-8

Contents

Dedication

Lovingly dedicated to

MAAIKE

my intimate friend and companion
who has taught me how to love, to laugh, and to play

Foreword

What a privilege it is for me to write this Foreword for Dr. Bryan Craig's new book, *Searching for Intimacy in Marriage.* I first encountered Bryan as a student in one of my Doctor of Ministry courses and immediately felt that he was a kindred spirit. His passion for helping Christians build stronger families and more effective marital relationships is contagious. I consider him to be an expert in this field—and not just in the southern hemisphere. He is also recognized as an expert in the United States as well. It is most appropriate, therefore, that he should now share some of his expertise through the medium of this book.

Marriages are in trouble worldwide. And the prognosis for marriage is not very good if one examines current trends in marital statistics. Marriage used to be the hallmark of stability—and the family the backbone of a secure society. Today it is rapidly becoming the antithesis of community. Many couples, and not just secular but Christian as well, are becoming fearful of the marriage bond. This is bad news in and of itself, but this isn't all. The really bad news is that a lot of marital and couple therapies today don't "cut the mustard"! They are just not that effective for confronting the forces operating today to undermine marriage.

Much therapy tends to focus too much on the teaching of superficial skills or the modification of marital bonds. This is why I believe that Bryan's emphasis here is so apposite. As his subtitle indicates, he highlights the important role that emotion plays in creating understanding and connectedness in the marital relationship. This is the "heart" of the matter. Couples have to connect at the level of their deepest emotions if marriage is to be successful over a lifetime.

My purpose here is not to review all that is written in this book—that would take another book in itself. I do want to emphasize, however, that Dr. Craig is a master at synthesizing critical research data and then presenting it in understandable concepts with practical suggestions for enhancing the marital bond. Throughout, he maintains a deeply spiritual emphasis. This book will not only be helpful to pastors and counselors—who carry the major burden for helping couples prepare for and then survive the challenges facing marriages today—but it will also help couples themselves who desire a better understanding of how they can enhance the intimacy of their relationship. My prayer is that God will bless the wisdom of this book to all who read it.

Archibald D. Hart, Ph.D., FPPR
Professor of Psychology and Dean Emeritus
Graduate School of Psychology
Fuller Theological Seminary

Introduction

Within every human heart is a yearning for intimacy, a deep desire for connection with other human beings. From the moment we are born, we crave the acceptance of others and long to be in relationship with them. Because intimacy is essential to our survival, we need always to know that someone is there for us. This quest for intimacy is well described by Anthony Welsh, who once said, "It is not the threat of death, illness, hardship, or poverty that crushes the human spirit; it is the fear of being alone and unloved in the universe."[1] We all desperately want to feel that we are loved, that we belong, and that we are part of community.

The fact is, we cannot be ourselves, by ourselves. We were made for community. Every one of us has an innate capacity for giving and receiving love and for responding to the people in our environment. We define who we are in the face of those people who constitute our community. Clearly, the way we come to think and feel about ourselves is fashioned and shaped by how we perceive the way others treat us. As Carolyn Saarni so aptly says, "We are the products of our relationships, which are always transactional . . . .We derive meaningfulness . . . from the people who have loved us, spent time with us, taught us, or spurned and perhaps even exploited us."[2]

In our search to find that meaningful relationship and to experience a sense of love and intimacy in our lives, most of us turn to marriage. This is where all social connectedness between people begins. In marriage, we crave the company and the self-affirmation that comes from our partner. We relish the deep and intimate connections and thrive on a companionship that embeds us in a cocoon of safety. Through receiving emotional support and nurture, we generate feelings of mutual trust, loyalty, and respect. Because of this, a good marriage has always been seen as the strongest predictor of personal happiness and well-being—the primary relationship that best satisfies our basic emotional needs. As a result, marriage is our most highly pursued relationship and a goal central to our lives.

The Changing Face of Marriage

Over the past forty years, our expectations regarding marriage have changed in response to the radical shift in values and beliefs that has occurred within society. As a result of rapid social, economic, and technological changes, individuals and couples have come to look on marriage differently now. Cultural historians tell us that it all began to unravel in the sixties when a whole generation of individuals fantasized about a great society of ideal love and pledged themselves to a world based on drugs, sex, and rock 'n roll. The seventies generation followed on by overdosing on everything that had been discovered in the sixties, and the eighties generation became the "Me Generation," with little sense of shared purpose or hope for a better society.

What these four decades spawned was a number of revolutionary movements that have impacted marriage and changed the face of the world in ways we are only just beginning to comprehend. The civil rights movement and the sexual revolution of the sixties and seventies, along with the feminist movement that grew out of the seventies and eighties, have radically changed the social rules, attitudes, and expectations that govern our personal lives. The way that men and women relate to each other will never be the same again. Added to this is an understanding of the way in which people embraced the dictums of the human potential movement during the eighties and nineties. These ideas and aspirations influenced us to be more self-absorbed and individualistic in our pursuits, and as a consequence, lose our sense of community and social consciousness.

As if this were not enough, we have all had to contend with the widespread impact of the information revolution. Through the use of cyberspace, new technologies are destabilizing our family life and work practices and transforming the ways we use to keep in touch with each other. What challenges us most is that these technologies are blurring the distinction between human interpersonal communication and the way in which information is transferred from one person to another. While time zones and distances may no longer be barriers to people networking with each other, the impersonal nature of these transactions may only serve to make us more independent and less caring and compassionate toward one another.

When you put all these influences together, you begin to grasp the enormity of the personal and social changes impacting our world and causing many to adopt new attitudes toward marriage and relationships. Whereas marriage used to be regarded as one of the visible symbols of stability, confidence, and optimism in our community, today it has lost a lot of its social importance and religious meaning. Today's generation, shaped by a new set of influences, is recreating marriage in its own image. Marriage is now preeminently a symbol of romantic love, with a focus on egalitarianism and mutual satisfaction.

This revolution in marriage is what Jack Dominian calls a "shift from social to emotional aptness." He suggests that contemporary marriages are focused not so much on "instrumentality, but on feelings and emotions" and that they feature a "companionate" relationship.

> The companionate variety emphasizes a male-female egalitarian partnership in which company, communication, support, healing, the exchange of feelings and sexual satisfaction are of paramount importance. It is no longer the discharge

of social roles but the quality of the relationship that matters. In a vague and ill-defined way, it is love that matters.[3]

This companionate relationship is no longer just about children, or families, or stability, or mutual comfort. It is primarily about the quality of the relationship between a man and a woman. And when the relationship is not working for one or both of the partners, this can very quickly be seen as the death-knell of the marriage.

With the development of these new attitudes and expectations, it is not surprising to find that the marriage relationship has now become quite fragile and that the divorce rate has risen to 40 percent. Many of the current generation of young couples have tried to accommodate and adjust to these widespread social and attitudinal changes and build good-quality relationships. But, without successful role models, this has been a difficult task. Many couples in a marital relationship appear to be struggling, despite the fact that they feel a greater sense of freedom to leave an unhappy marriage.

In reflecting on the changes occurring in marriages and relationships, it is natural for us to want to lament and wring our hands over the fragility of the marriage institution or the gloomy statistics that indicate how marriage has lost its meaning in our world.

However, there are several ways that we can look at this situation. We can either decry the decay in one of our important social institutions and see these phenomena as evil and sinister, or we can accept that these changes are the inevitable consequence of social, cultural, and economic growth and development. If we are more accepting of these changes, then we may choose to see the present dilemma as an opportunity to rethink and redefine our attitudes toward marriage.

It may also provide us with the motivation to reexamine and reconstruct a meaningful and coherent view of marriage for the twenty-first century. Certainly, many of the changes that have taken place in the past forty years are here to stay, and winding back the clock is not an option.

The Role That Emotion Plays in Developing Marital Intimacy

It is the purpose of this book to explore and understand the nature of marriage and what makes it work—and to identify what we mean when we say that we are "in love." It seeks to examine those processes by which a couple establish a strong emotional bond with each other and achieve a sense of intimacy in their marital relationship. It also outlines some of the common barriers that prevent couples from finding the emotional closeness and support so essential to maintaining a long-term, intimate love relationship.

In 1999 the Australian Institute of Family Studies released a working paper entitled "Toward Understanding the Reasons for Divorce," which highlighted some interesting results from a national survey indicating that marriages stand or fall according to strength of the emotional bonds between the partners. This research revealed that the majority of those who had experienced divorce cited that the main reason for the demise of their relationship was that they were unsatisfied with the affective qualities of their relationship.[4] They clearly recognized that their lack of intimacy and emotional closeness with their partner was the major contributing factor that had led to the end of their relationship.

These findings are significant, because they highlight the key role that emotional attachments play in the development of intimacy in marriage. In fact, several prominent researchers have recently stressed the importance of conceptualizing adult intimacy as an emotional bond and have called for marital therapists to recognize the crucial part that emotions play in intimate relationships.[5] Emotions, they assert, are clearly a vital part of the responses that marital partners make to each other—responses that form the building blocks of interactional patterns in the marriage.

John Gottman's research suggests that "emotionally intelligent" marriages are those that work not because the couple are "smarter, richer, or more psychologically astute than others," but that they are "more in touch with their emotions" and better able "to understand, honor, and respect each other and their marriage."[6] Every couple, he believes, creates in their own marriage and family relationships a unique culture about emotion as they deal with the exchange of positive and negative emotions. These exchanges of emotion are what he calls the "hidden emotional dynamics of marriage" or "the invisible forces that hold a marriage together or tear it apart."[7]

Furthermore, studies have clearly shown that emotion is a key to understanding the development of marital distress and dysfunction. Gottman's studies of the physiological arousal of couples in conflict have provided a very powerful argument for the primary importance of understanding and focusing on emotion in intimate relationships.[8]

What is clear from the research is that most attempts by individuals to control, avoid, or manipulate emotion inevitably create some kind of relational problems. When people have difficulty processing, articulating, or regulating their own emotions or connecting with the emotions in others, there are usually significant implications for the relationship. If feelings are not acknowledged, they cannot be addressed. So researchers are suggesting that a very successful way to improve troubled relationships and enhance individual functioning is to focus on working with the emotional or affective processes of the relationship.

The point is that the emotional dimension of life lies at the very heart of all relationships and that any attempt to improve the level of intimacy in a marriage must focus on the way a couple connect with each other emotionally. Our emotions are the heart and soul of who we are, and they play a vital role in the process of attachment that leads to the development, maintenance, or deterioration of our relationships. Our emotions monitor the status of our needs and goals, they drive us to get what we want and to avoid what we do not want, and they profoundly influence the meaning and purpose we attribute to our lives and our relationships. They shape our personality and serve as the connection between our beliefs, values, ideas, and feelings. Through our emotions, we respond to others, bond with them, and communicate to them our needs and longings.

While it may seem that all this discussion is somewhat academic, we need to remind ourselves that for far too long the part that emotions play in marriage and in the development of the marriage relationship has largely been ignored. We have avoided talking about the emotional realm and often overlooked the whole issue of the importance and power that emotional connection plays in relationships.

What is more, the Christian church has for centuries been very suspicious of emotions and regarded them as "spoilers" that sabotage and overwhelm the intellect, creating obstacles to responsible and holy living. The church has subscribed to what some have called the "doctrine of rational supremacy," which asserts that emotion and passion must be brought under the control of reason and rationality.[9] This belief, which has been so dominant in Christian circles, has been used to suggest that a person who acts on impulse or is emotional is either irrational, eccentric, or "out of his mind."

By stressing the importance of rational decision making in its ministry to individuals, couples, and families, the church has often failed to acknowledge the significant part that the emotional life plays in the bonding or attachment processes that form the heart of true intimacy in marriage. This comes on top of the fact that men and boys are taught by society not to show their weakness or deny their masculinity by giving expression to their emotions. Experience shows just how devastating this can be to intimacy levels in a marriage.

Many couples who attend church and community-presented marriage education programs or marriage enrichment seminars have given evidence of just how much they are struggling to deal with the emotional side of their marriage and, as a result, failing to connect or bond effectively with their partner. Couples often know little about their own emotions, mainly because they have not learned how to effectively identify, own, connect with, and process their own emotional responses. Consequently, many relationships flounder or at best plateau or stagnate, rarely achieving a satisfying level of intimacy.

An Important Strategy for the Church

Certainly a key strategy for improving many marriages between Christian partners would be for them to learn how to develop and maintain an intimate love relationship. In particular, couples need to be made aware of the crucial role of emotion in marriage and how it is the key to intimacy and connection. They need to understand how emotional closeness is developed through effective communication with one another and how they can successfully deal with the emotional component in marital conflict.

This presentation has been prepared specifically to address the need for the Adventist Church to be more intentional in its ministry to couples. In the past, the Church has not taken seriously enough the impact that social change has had upon people's lives and the way in which individual attitudes and lifestyles practices have changed as a result. It has not sought to confront, in any real depth, changing attitudes toward marriage and relationships in ways that approach or challenge the thought processes of the post-modern mind. It is time for the church to recognize more than ever that the subjective, pragmatic, and fragmented nature of our post-modern world provides the church with a wonderful opportunity to say something relevant and meaningful to couples who are looking for value and certainty in a world that has become quite uncertain and confusing.

Surely the time has come for the Church to emphasize those components essential for creating and sustaining a good, satisfying marriage. By presenting the biblical view that marriage is a companionship and working partnership based on notions of mutual commitment, personal responsibility, and social accountability, the ministry of the church can provide effective nurture and guidance in an age of uncertainty and discontinuity.

Emotionally Focused Marital Education

The major objective of this work is to provide a resource of material about marriage that can be used to inform and educate married partners and those preparing for marriage about the processes and skills involved in building a healthy, happy, secure, and stable marriage relationship. The approach outlined in this material has been called Emotionally Focused Marriage Education, because it sees the emotional connections between marriage partners as the primary pathway through which intimacy, understanding, and a sense of closeness develop in marriage. It targets emotion not only as the gateway to marital growth and development but as the most effective avenue to bringing about change in the relationship. By focusing largely on the emotional aspects of their relationship, couples are encouraged to develop an emotionally intelligent marriage. This is achieved when the two learn how to be more emotionally competent and responsive to each other by first being in touch with their own feelings—and then being able to understand and connect with their partner at the emotional level.

Emotionally Focused Marital Education grows out of concepts developed by Susan Johnson in *Creating Connection: The Practice of Emotionally Focused Marital Therapy*.[10] Unlike marital therapy, Emotionally Focused Marital Education is not about creating change in the marital relationship but about creating awareness and insight, and the learning of those skills necessary for marital growth and change. In this sense it is a preventative approach to marriage that helps couples generate an inner awareness of their own strengths and weaknesses and develop an understanding of how the emotional bonding process works. It also seeks to highlight ways couples can generate powerful new emotional events and experiences.

This Emotionally Focused approach to educating people about marriage and the development of intimacy in their marital relationship is based on the following ideas and beliefs:

1. Love and the Process of Emotional Bonding

The focus in this marital education model is on understanding adult love as the development of emotional ties, or the process of attachment, that develops secure bonds between two people. It seeks to understand how this process occurs, and it stresses the part that emotional accessibility and responsiveness play in the building of these bonds. It also highlights the importance that the skills of empathy and validation play in creating feelings of security, comfort, and connectedness for each marriage partner. It acknowledges that people actively process and construct their perceptions and experiences of themselves, the other person, and their mutual relationship through the interactions they share together.

2. The Importance of Emotion

Emotionally Focused Marital Education focuses on the importance of emotion as the key to fostering the creation of attachment bonds. It recognizes that it is through our emotions that we discover what matters most to us and what meaning we place on particular events and experiences. It begins with a focus on self-awareness and the need to develop emotional competence and confidence through listening to, managing, and resolving one's own feelings. It recognizes that a poor self-image can hold individuals back from being emotionally and spiritually alive and from contributing positively to a relationship.

This approach does not ignore or overlook the fact that attachment bonds between people consist of behavioral, cognitive, and emotional elements, but rather chooses to make its focus on emotional responses a matter of priority. The reason this model emphasizes emotional responses and expressions is because they constitute the primary signaling system used by intimate partners to activate and orient themselves toward each other and organize and motivate their bonding or attachment behaviors.

3. Focus on the Process of Interaction

As a way of understanding and relieving marital distress, the focus in this model is placed on identifying rigid and destructive interactional patterns, acknowledging and regulating their compelling negative effect, and accessing and processing the emotional responses and specific emotional triggers that occur between the couple in conflict. This approach to marital distress recognizes that problems tend to be self maintaining and occur when partners keep repeating the same old vicious cycles, disown feelings or aspects of themselves, or try to construct unhelpful ways to resolve their insecurities. Emphasis is placed on creating emotional engagement by the recognition and validation of individual needs for security, protection, comfort, or connection as a way of reducing distress and regulating negative emotions. Stress is also placed on creating new and more positive experiences that deepens intimacy and strengthen bonding.

4. Investing in Positive Bonding Experiences

Another focus of this approach to marital education is on the need for couples to intentionally create powerful new bonding events or moments by being accessible and responsive to each other. This action constitutes the basis for building and reinforcing secure bonds. Couples are also encouraged to see the importance of developing strong social networks (community) that support personal and relational health and well-being and strengthen the level of intimacy they experience.

The material contained in this book is divided into four distinct sections. The first section explores the biblical or theological understanding of marriage and the way in which we all yearn for intimacy in relationship. Special attention is given to the nature and purpose of marriage as expressed by the Creator-God when He instituted marriage at the beginning of human history. Emphasis is also given to the process of bonding and how we socially construct our understanding of love.

The second section examines two important ways that intimacy is achieved in marriage. First, it focuses on the way in which the process of communication contributes to emotional closeness and marital intimacy—and then highlights the part that sexual intimacy plays in the achievement of marital satisfaction and fulfillment. The third section looks at the major obstacles to marital intimacy and discusses ways to overcome these emotional blockages. The focus in this section is on dealing with conflict and outlining ways to cope with hurt, anger, depression, grief, and stress in the marriage relationship.

SEARCHING FOR INTIMACY IN MARRIAGE

The final section of the book outlines some practical suggestions and biblical guidelines for increasing intimacy in marriage. A number of positive strategies are given to assist couples in recognizing and preventing marital burnout—and in achieving optimal levels of intimacy in their marital relationship.

Notes:

1. Paul Pearsall, *A Healing Intimacy* (New York: Crown Trade Paperbacks, 1994).

2. Carolyn Saarni, *The Development of Emotional Competence* (New York: Guilford Press, 1999), p. 9.

3. Jack Dominian, *Marriage* (London: Heinemann, 1995), p. 5.

4. Ilene Wolcott and Jody Hughes, *Toward Understanding the Reasons for Divorce* (Australian Institute of Family Studies, Working Paper No. 20, 1999), p. 8.

5. Susan M. Johnson and Leslie S. Greenberg, *The Heart of the Matter* (New York: Brunner/Mazel, 1994), p. 3.

6. John Gottman and Nan Silver, *The Seven Principles for Making Marriage Work* (New York: Crown Publishers, Inc., 1999), pp. 3, 4.

7. John Gottman, *Why Marriages Succeed or Fail* (New York: Simon and Schuster, 1994), p. 26.

8. John Gottman and Nan Silver, *The Seven Principles for Making Marriage Work*, pp. 36-42.

9. Johnson and Greenberg, *The Heart of the Matter*, pp. 173, 174.

10. Susan M. Johnson, *Creating Connection: The Practice of Emotionally Focused Martial Therapy* (New York: Brunner/Mazel, 1996), pp. 1-24.

ONE

Intimacy—the Goal of Marriage

A biblical understanding of the nature of marriage has been lost on many people today. Since the 1960s, high divorce rates and the increasing amount of marital breakdown, especially in western culture, has led many to rethink their attitude toward marriage. Not that marriage is unpopular. Clearly, it is not! An overwhelming majority of individuals still aspires to be married at some stage in their life.[1] But what is changing are the attitudes and expectations people have about marriage. Whereas in the past, people got married for economic survival, today the reasons individuals pursue marriage are more about personal fulfillment and emotional support.[2]

In this changing social context, where individualism and subjectivism dominate, what people seem to lack are really effective role models and an adequate understanding of the nature and purpose of marriage. The old ways of looking at marriage and relationships are simply not attractive or acceptable. But there are no new or different models of marriage that have stood the test of time to instruct us. From a Christian point of view, this provides the church with a significant opportunity to clearly articulate the relevance of the biblical perspective on God's plan and purpose for instituting marriage and to apply it to the current social context.

Marriage was God's idea from the beginning of human history. When He created Adam and Eve on the sixth day of creation, He immediately placed them into a relationship with each other as husband and wife (Genesis 1:26, 27; 2:18-25). From the biblical record, it is clear that God intended that this marriage would be the pattern for all future marriage relationships. Furthermore, the Gospel writers indicate that centuries later, Jesus endorsed God's original concept of marriage and instructed individuals and couples to embrace a proper understanding of its nature and purpose.

> "Haven't you read in your Bible that the Creator originally made man and woman for each other, male and female? And because of this, a man *leaves* father and mother and is *firmly bonded* to his wife, *becoming one flesh*—no longer two bodies but one." Because God created this organic union of the two sexes, no one should desecrate his art by cutting them apart (Matthew 19:4-6, *THE MESSAGE,* emphasis supplied).

The apostle Paul in his ministry to the early Christian church also believed that marriage was a special relationship created by God. Because he valued marriage as a divine gift, he admonished the believers to safeguard its sanctity by protecting and honoring it with their highest esteem: "Honour marriage, and guard the sacredness of sexual intimacy between wife and husband" (Hebrews 13:4, *THE MESSAGE*). He supported the idea that marriage represented the closest and most intimate relationship between a man and woman, and in his letter to the embattled and divided church at Ephesus, he used it as an analogy of the union that exists between Christ and His Church. Ephesians 5:21-33.

Marriage As an Expression of the Relational Nature of God

The Apostle Paul says that "by taking a long and thoughtful look at what God has created, people have always been able to see...the mystery of His Divine being" (Romans 1:19, 20, *THE MESSAGE*). This would suggest that when we study the nature of the marriage relationship, we should learn something about who

God is and what He is like. It might also help us to understand and connect with the deep yearning of His heart and appreciate why He created marriage. By observing His great handiwork, we catch a glimpse of His character, personality, and motivations.

Marriage is a beautiful reflection of the heart of God. At the institution of marriage in the Garden of Eden, the Creator fashioned and shaped human beings in His image and according to His likeness. Genesis 1:26. His creative act reveals how He placed in both Adam and Eve a capacity for giving and receiving love within the confines of a loving and committed relationship. This marital relationship highlighted the importance that God places on intimacy, harmony, and relatedness—and shows how His relational nature is mirrored in the self-giving love of two individuals who find a sense of unity and togetherness through the joy of marital love.

A wider survey of the scriptures helps us develop an even greater understanding of just how much God longs to be in relationship with His created beings and how much the marriage relationship is an expression of His relational nature. The personalized images and descriptions of God presented by the various Bible writers provide us with many vignettes that reveal His nature and personality. The apostle John declares that "God is love" and that "love comes from God" (1 John 4:7, 8, *THE MESSAGE*). He says that "everyone who loves is born of God and experiences a relationship with God."

God's nature is that of *agape*—a self-giving love. This is exemplified in the essence of self-giving, which finds expression through the harmonious and loving fellowship of the three persons of the Trinity as they relate to each other. It is revealed in the loving and liberating initiative of the incarnation, in which Jesus sought to restore agape-love relationships. "This is my command," Jesus said, "that you love one another the way I loved you" (John 15:12, *THE MESSAGE*). He taught that we find our greatest fulfilment when we love God "with all our passion and prayer and intelligence and when we love others as well as we love ourselves" (Matthew 22:37-39, *THE MESSAGE*).

Donald Messer, in his book *A Conspiracy of Goodness*, presents a picture of God as a Lover. He sees God imaged in the Song of Songs as a passionate bridegroom who actively pursues, attracts, and entreats His bride. In the Gospels, the passion of Jesus is not seen as passive and indifferent but rather as a deep, committed love that agonizes for those He loves and for whom He suffers. Clearly, Jesus was pained over the disconnection, estrangement, and rejection He experienced in relationship with this world.

Other biblical passages portray God as a Friend who delights in openly disclosing Himself to others and actively seeks to form close, intimate relationships with those He calls His friends. "I'm no longer calling you servants," Jesus said, "No, I've named you friends, because I've let you in on everything I've heard from the Father" (John 15:15, *THE MESSAGE*). Jesus' relationship with others was not a self-absorbed, exclusive friendship that flowed from a position of superiority but one that issued from a sensitive and empathic heart that felt the joy, pain, and discouragement of others. His fraternizing with the nonentities and ordinary people in His society, even visiting and eating with the poor, the weak, and the outcasts, highlighted how much He sought to establish a genuine connection with others based on equality and mutuality.

To suggest that God is a distant and remote being is to deny the reality of who God is and what He is like! Alienation and loneliness are qualities foreign to God's own environment. They have never been a part of His nature. That is why—when He created human beings as male and female—He said that it was "not good for [them] to be alone" (Genesis 2:18). Rather than commit them to isolation and alienation, God deliberately placed them in an intimately satisfying interpersonal relationship. Genesis 1:26; 2:18, 24. The affective or emotional side of God is clearly apparent in the way He relates to shame and brokenness.

The psalmist David speaks of the Lord being "close to the broken-hearted" and willing to listen to anyone who is crying out for help (Psalm 34:17, 18, NIV). He images God as "gracious in everything He does" and willing to "give a hand to those down on their luck." He is a true friend who "sticks by all who love Him," lavishing them with His grace and favour (Psalm 145:14, 17, 21, *THE MESSAGE*).

God's emotional support is never far from those wounded by the mistrust, hostility, and estrangement so typical of human relationships, even from the earliest times. Aware of the tragic outcomes that sin has bought and the pervasive effect it has had on human relationships, God has always been quick to invest Himself in the ongoing work of forgiving, healing, and restoring broken relationships. Jesus called on His followers to recover their lives through putting their faith and confidence in God. The apostle Paul commanded the believers to follow Christ and put all "sexual promiscuity, impurity, lust,…bad temper, irritability, meanness, profanity and dirty talk" out of their lives (Colossians 3:5-7, *THE MESSAGE*)—and to put on the "new life of love" characterized by "compassion, kindness, humility, quiet strength, discipline, being even tempered, being content with second place [and being] quick to forgive an offence" (Colossians 3:12, 13, *THE MESSAGE*).

In establishing marriage, God, true to His nature, has fashioned and shaped a relationship based on love and intimacy that meets the human need for mutuality, co-creation, and friendship. With a capacity for loving and a need for relatedness, Adam and Eve were nothing less than a reflection of their Creator's own relational nature—and as such, they bought glory to Him. Having recognized that is was "not good" for them to exist alone, God created a marriage and then pronounced it "very good" (Genesis 1:31, NIV).

Marriage As a Journey Toward Intimacy

The model of marriage presented in Genesis 2:24, 25 (NIV) outlines clearly God's original plan and purpose for marriage:

> For this reason [aloneness, verse 18] a man will leave his father and mother and be united to his wife, and they will become one flesh. The man and his wife were both naked and they felt no shame

The way God instituted the marriage relationship between Adam and Eve is highly significant. The introductory words *therefore* or *for this reason* (verse 24) indicated that God was holding up this relationship as the pattern for marriage for all future generations. The phrase *the man and his wife* (verse 25) implies that the marriage He established was a monogamous, heterosexual relationship shared exclusively by two married partners.

In this scriptural passage we also find a description of the way in which Adam and Eve were brought together in a covenant relationship. The words of verse 24 provide a clear and concise outline of the major elements of the marriage relationship and the actual process whereby a husband and wife journey together toward the achievement of a sense of oneness. The expression *become one flesh* clearly indicates that companionship and intimacy constitute the goal of marriage. Through the partnership established in the marital relationship, God has ordained the means whereby a deep and lasting friendship can be achieved by two people who choose to remain committed to each other. More than any other human relationship, the friendship achieved through marriage comes closest to touching the image and likeness of God in human form.[3]

Three Key Expressions That Shape Our View of Marriage

In our quest for understanding more fully the biblical concept of marriage, let us now examine the three key expressions in Genesis 2:24. We should also observe how the nuances contained in these three expressions give us a greater understanding and appreciation of the dynamic forces that influence and shape the biblical view of marriage. These three expressions highlight the three key components to building a balanced view of marriage and illuminate the pathway to developing a happy, healthy marital relationship.

1. Mutual desire and attraction. In the first instance, Genesis 2:24 says: "For this reason a man will *leave.*" The Hebrew word for "leave" is *azab*. This is a forceful term that literally means "to forsake or abandon" and is frequently used to describe Israel's act of forsaking Yahweh for false Gods.[4] In the patriarchal society, the idea of a man leaving his father and mother, to whom he had the most sacred obligation and social responsibility, was a startling and revolutionary thought. But here verse 24 overturns this idea and declares unambiguously that a man's first loyalty is to his wife. So what the Bible is suggesting is that both men and women are to leave—to cut loose from those ties or bonds of solidarity with their parents. Maintaining these kinship ties can in fact encroach upon the independence and freedom of the marriage relationship and inhibit the couple's ability to be loyal to each other—especially the man to his wife.[5]

What the "leaving" of Genesis 2:24 infers is that it is absolutely necessary for the couple to be free from any outside interference as they pursue the development of their emotional and sexual relationship. They are to sever themselves from those familial ties that restrict their independence and prevent the establishment of very clear relationship boundaries. This process of differentiation will enable the couple as marital partners to establish a very special identity of their own, distinct and separate from their families of origin. Without this sense of separateness, the marriage relationship may easily be sabotaged by outside influences. However, that does not mean that the couple loses all sense of connectedness with their families. Not at all. They must seek to maintain a good healthy balance between separateness and connectedness.

This act of "leaving" on the part of the man (and the woman too) is clearly motivated by the desire for companionship and a sense of connectedness with each other. Genesis 2:18 says that God created the woman to be a "helper suited to his needs," thus implying that as equal partners in the marriage, both the man and his wife were not only suited to, but capable of, meeting each other's physical, emotional, social, and spiritual needs. It is also obvious that this is "the reason" (verse 24) why they mutually desire each other and are drawn into relatedness with one another.

Furthermore, it is apparent from the narrative that Adam greets the introduction of the woman (verse 23) not as a benign, disinterested spectator but as an individual highly attracted and motivated toward her. Adam freely and passionately embraces her as one who offers the prospect of companionship, partnership, and sexual fulfilment. To overlook the suitability of the woman to meet all of Adam's needs and to deny his absolute delight at the attractiveness of her presence, availability, and responsiveness to him, is to miss the impact of that first meeting: "This is now bone of my bones and flesh of my flesh; she shall be called woman, for she was taken out of man" (verse 23).

2. Mutual commitment. The second element in the process of marriage formation involves the concept of union. The Hebrew word for "be united" (verse 24) is the verb *dabaq*. This is another robust term. It signifies a "strong personal attachment."[6] The original imagery of the word implies "clinging, sticking, remaining physically close, as a girdle to the loin or as skin to flesh and flesh to bone."[7] It is often used as a technical covenant term for the bonding of Israel to the Lord[8] and implies an agreement of deep and lasting significance that involves the totality of two parties to the agreement. Furthermore, *dabaq* especially emphasizes the inward, attitudinal dimensions of the covenant bond—attitudes expressed in the total commitment of the marital partners to each other and to their relationship. It "implies a devotion and an unshakeable faith between two humans; it connotes a permanent attraction that transcends genital union, to which nonetheless it gives meaning."[9]

The apostle Paul elaborates further on this theme in Ephesians 5. In this chapter he suggests that the deeply spiritual relationship that exists between a husband and wife is one in which they are both devoted to each other in a "mutual submission" (verse 21) that ennobles, nourishes, and gives strength to the marriage relationship. This submission is characterized by a devotion of love and self-surrender that is in no way demeaning for either the man or the woman but rather an expression of the grateful acceptance of the care and support they enjoy from each other. This mutual gratitude is reflected well in the words of Markus Barth, who says, "Paul is thinking of a voluntary, free, joyful and thankful partnership"[10] between the marital partners who are joined together in a relationship in which they are the "source" of each other's love, nurture, and support. Ephesians 5:23, 25.

Paul then proceeds to emphasize the closeness of the union between the husband and wife by quoting the words of Genesis 2:24, in which the verb *cleave* or "closely united" literally means "to be glued to." Here he endorses the Hebrew concept that marriage is not a half-hearted, transient, short-term commitment but an extremely close, binding relationship between two people. This mutual commitment is a basic element in the Christian concept of marriage that is based not only on "leaving" but also on a deep respect for each other and a desire to "meet each other's needs" (Genesis 2:18). It does not suggest that the marital partners in any way lose or give up their individuality in order to achieve intimacy. In reality, the quality of their relationship is built around the fact that both have a strong sense of self or personhood, and it is this personal strength that they bring the marriage.

3. Mutual intimacy and companionship. The third and final element involved in the establishment of the marriage relationship is highlighted by the expression *basar chad*—or "become one flesh." The term *basar* or "flesh" in the Old Testament refers not only to the physical body but to a person's whole existence in the world.[11] By "one flesh" is meant a mutual dependence and reciprocity in all areas of life,"[12] a uniting that embraces the natural lives of two persons in their entirety,"[13] a "sexual concourse and a psychological concurrence, in the fullest sense of conjunction of bodies and minds, at once through eros and agape...a psychic as well as physiological gift of loyalty and exchange."[14]

So while we certainly acknowledge that the *one flesh* relationship involves the sexual union of the husband and wife, this is by no means all that is included in the meaning of this biblical expression. The use of the term *one flesh* in both the Old and New Testaments clearly indicates a "oneness and intimacy in the total relationship of the whole person of the husband and the whole person of the wife."[15] It is this concept that lies at the very heart of what God intended the marriage relationship to achieve, and it encapsulates the goal of marriage—intimacy and companionship.

However, we must hasten to add that Genesis 2:24 does not imply that this one-fleshness is an instantaneously achieved state. The phrase "they shall be one flesh" is better translated "they shall *become* one flesh." Marriage is a process of becoming—a relationship that grows, deepens, and strengthens over time. As Samuel Terrien points out: "The Hebrew nuance, not usually conveyed in the English translations, indicates that this state...results from a process of development that deepens in intensity and strengthens itself with the passage of time instead of dissipating like a straw fire."[16] This helpful insight invites us to see marriage as a relationship between two people that grows and develops through the various stages of the family life cycle. Many social researchers have observed how all marriages tend to adapt and change as they pass through the normal, predictable crises and stages of development on the pathway toward maturity and wholeness.

Furthermore, Terrien's comments suggest that marriage is about two people who, through the process of growth and change, begin to realize more and more the personal and relational potential inherent in their relationship. Through the affectional ties or bonds established within the marital relationship, the couple begins to generate a capacity for intimacy and friendship that releases their potential and inspires them toward psychological maturity and emotional and spiritual health. There are further implications that emerge from this third expression, "they shall become one flesh." The concept of unity is stressed by the use of the word *one*. Not that God intended that a married couple would become one in number and live in an enmeshed symbiotic relationship or become like Siamese twins. No! What is clear from the use of "one" throughout scripture is that the notion of becoming "one flesh" is meant to convey the idea of unity, connectedness, and caring.[17] Jesus spoke of Himself as being "one" with the Father (John 17:11), and He prayed for His disciples "that they may be one" just "as we [Father] are one, I in them and you in me, may they be brought to complete unity" (John 17:22, 23).

The early church, in Acts 4:32, is also described as being "one in heart and mind," suggesting that the Christian believers enjoyed a sense of harmony, unity, and equality.[18] So being "one" in the marital sense denotes the idea that two people develop a sense of intimacy and connectedness through the complete unity of their beings (physically, emotionally, and spiritually) while at the same time maintaining the integrity and separateness of their individual selves. There is unity in diversity.

Another nuance clearly implicit in the concept of "one" is, as suggested above, the idea of equality. In the creation of Adam and Eve, God has stated that their relationship was to provide for a mutual companionship based on their equality as persons. This equality is indicated in two specific expressions God used in describing Eve. In the first instance He said that Eve, as Adam's partner, would be a "helper suitable for him" (Genesis 2:18, NIV). The English word *helper* is translated from the Hebrew *ezer* and does not imply that Eve was inferior, subordinate, or subservient to Adam or that she was to be his servant or aide.[19] On the contrary, *ezer* is one who provides physical, emotional, and spiritual sustenance for the loved one (Deuteronomy 33:7, 26, 29; Psalm 70:5; 121:1, 2) and is often used to describe God Himself!

The second expression—"suitable"—is translated from the Hebrew word *kneqdwo*, which is based on the term *neged*, meaning "corresponding to." The addition of a prefix (k) and a suffix (d) to the word *neged* indicates that a comparison is being made between the two individuals and suggests that Eve, as *knegdwo*, is similar to Adam and that she is equal and adequate for him. In other words, they were created as equal partners capable of developing a warm and loving relationship with each other, because they were similar, yet different—companions able to meet each other's needs.[20] The biblical text gives no evidence that Adam and Eve therefore believed that either of them was superior in either power, status, or skill. The intimacy they were to achieve was made possible because they were equals. True intimacy is only ever possible between two people where there is a genuine equality of personhood.

The concept of "one flesh" is a unique and fascinating expression that God uses to describe the intimacy of the marriage relationship. Often the idea of "one flesh" is taken to imply simply the physical, sexual union that occurs between a husband and wife. Perhaps this is because of the meaning given to the word "flesh" in English, but in both the Old and New Testaments, the word *flesh* has a wider meaning. Frequently in scripture, the Hebrew (*basar*) and the Greek (*sarks*) words for "flesh" are used to designate all living things or human beings and are not specifically used as sexual terms. In fact, except for one reference in the Old Testament (Ecclesiastics 2:8), the word *flesh* carries no sexual connotation at all. Generally, it refers to the whole being and denotes the complete physical, emotional, and spiritual aspects of a person's being as they live their lives throughout the course of their earthly existence.

John Bristow says that although Jesus never defined the phrase "one flesh," we can make seven important observations about the wording.[21] First, becoming "one flesh" does not imply that two individual personalities are meant to merge into one in order for a husband and a wife to become a whole person. Second, becoming "one flesh" does not mean that marriage partners will always agree on everything but rather affirm their "differentness." Third, becoming "one flesh" implies an attachment or bonding that results in them being "one" in terms of their hopes, drives, and ambition—and that they are headed together in the same direction.

Fourth, he suggests that becoming "one flesh" implies that a couple become emotionally responsive to each other, connect with each other's feelings, and communicate with each other a sense of joy and pain, happiness and hurts. Fifth, becoming "one flesh" rules out the idea that a marriage is composed of superior over an inferior—or that the needs, choices, or ambitions of one are more important than those of the other. There is a sense of gender equality. Sixth, becoming "one flesh" is a process that requires time and experience to achieve. And last, that becoming "one flesh" has a spiritual dimension. It describes a relationship that God created and blessed and that He intended would be a permanent, life-long partnership.

In Genesis 2:25, the scriptural record appears to underscore the means by which this intimacy or "oneness" is achieved. Verse 25 indicates that this pristine couple were both "naked" and knew "no shame." The Hebrew word for "naked" is *arom,* which implies that they were both open to each other, innocent and trusting. They were exposed to one another without fear of criticism or rejection.[22] This level of intimacy was only possible because they truly loved and trusted one another and were not afraid to be totally authentic and transparent with each other. They clearly accepted that they were equals and that this affirmation of their personhood became the basis for the unity and companionship they experienced together.

Marriage As a Covenant Relationship

Throughout the scriptures, marriage is presented both as a covenant—and as a covenant relationship. Malachi, the Old Testament prophet, clearly referred to marriage as a covenant when he declared, "she is your partner, the wife of your marriage covenant" (Malachi 2:14, NIV). Using the unfaithfulness of his own wife as a backdrop for a discussion of God's love for His people, Hosea pictures God as a Lover pursuing His fickle bride and seeking to woo and reconcile her back into a covenantal relationship (Hosea 2:18, 19).

The Hebrew words *azab* and *dabaq* used in Genesis 2:24 to describe the relationship between Adam and Eve clearly indicate a covenant context. Both words are associated with covenant making and evoke so many strong images of bonding, attachment to another, total commitment, and permanence in relationship. The language used here not only parallels the "oath of solidarity" and the language of "covenant partnership"[23] but indicates that Adam was expressing to Eve an attitude of devotion and commitment to the marriage relationship. The covenantal connotations of these words must also be seen in the light of their usage elsewhere in scripture, such as with Israel's being "joined to" God in covenant faithfulness and in a relationship that God intended would be binding and permanent. So it must be understood that the language of the covenant was essentially the language of commitment,[24] and it was hoped that friendship and affection would grow out of the covenantal relationship over time. Anything less than total commitment would inevitably harm the covenant relationship and make the obligations of the agreement burdensome.[25]

A covenant agreement involved a reciprocal promise or pledge made by two partners to demonstrate exclusive love, loyalty, and devotion to one another as long as they were both alive.[26] Furthermore, it implied that specific rights, obligations, and promises needed to be maintained so that the couple could enjoy a binding and lasting relationship. The marriage covenant was based on a love that enabled both the husband and wife to accept each other unconditionally, to share in one another's pain and sorrows, and to rejoice in each other's victories and accomplishments. The apostle Paul describes the kind of love necessary for the marriage covenant to succeed, in 1 Corinthians 13:4-7, *THE MESSAGE:*

> Love never gives up. Loves cares more for others than for self. Love doesn't want what it doesn't have. Love doesn't strut, doesn't have a swelled head, doesn't force itself on others, isn't always "me first," doesn't fly off the handle, doesn't keep score of the sins of others, doesn't revel when others grovel, takes pleasure in the flowering of truth, puts up with anything, trusts God always, always looks for the best, never looks back, but keeps going to the end. Love never dies.

Loren Wade suggests that there are a number of significant meanings inherent in the Old Testament concept of covenant that impact on our understanding of marriage. The five nuances that he reflects on are:

1. Chosenness—a concept that filled the respondent with a sense of awe and humble gratitude at being chosen.

2. Belonging—a concept that placed emphasis not on individuality but on deriving a sense of personal identity from solidarity with another.

3. Separateness—a concept that suggests an exclusiveness in one's devotion to another. Here there is no room for rivals—only total commitment to the covenant partner.

4. Knowledge—a concept that suggests a relational dimension, a knowing of another, not just intellectually but experientially.

5. Faithfulness—a concept that implies a love-inspired loyalty and steadfastness. A love that aspires to permanence. [27]

Marriage After the Fall

Most of the preceding discussion about the beliefs and core values enunciated by God at the institution of marriage clearly indicates His original intention for marriage and the process that He saw would be involved in the achievement of an intimate, long-term relationship. But this ideal expressed so succinctly in Genesis 2:18-25 was soon shattered. The entrance of sin in Genesis 3 highlights the devastating effects that resulted when Adam and Eve turned their backs on God and each other and walked out of the covenant relationship they had learned to enjoy. With the experience of sin, or a broken relationship (Isaiah 59:2-4), human nature was altered, and the relationship between male and female, husband and wife, irrevocably changed.

Once equals, co-regents over the earth (Genesis 1:26-30), the Edenic couple now experienced disconnectedness, a loss of integrity, and a distortion of their gender identities. The delicate alignment, the joy of interdependence, was disrupted, and the dance *of* intimacy spoken of so concisely and meaningfully was now replaced by the dance *for* intimacy. Human innocence had been destroyed by the intrusion of self-interest, defensiveness, and denial, and the balance and unity in the marriage partnership were severely affected. Adam and Eve had lost the "oneness" which they had known with their Creator-God and with each other (Genesis 3:6-24).

This radical change in their relationship created a need for them to be highly dependent on each other. Something had happened that made it much more difficult for them to be interdependent and to meet each other's needs. They struggled to support each other in their woundedness and brokenness. Their relationship now became marked by fear, anxiety, and pain. They experienced themselves as disconnected and distant from each other and as wanting to hide from God (Genesis 3:10). Naked and exposed to one another's taunting and blaming, they found themselves motivated by guilt and crushed by their sense of shame and humiliation.

What a tragic description this is of the human condition and the dilemma into which the whole human race has been plunged. As a result of Adam and Eve's fall, human beings now struggle with a sense of isolation, fragmentation, and oppression that flows from their loss of dignity, esteem, and connectedness. Ray Anderson expresses it well when he says:

> The loss of identity and personal dignity was no doubt communicated from generation to generation as a sense of shame and isolation. One of the deepest wounds to the human spirit is the isolation and fragmentation that occurs when self-dignity and self-worth are systematically eroded. This is the pervasive effect of any form of human bondage and oppression, whether it be due to race, economic factors, political control, or marital and family abuse.[28]

The story in Genesis 3 highlights further how Adam and Eve's marriage suffered as a result of their woundedness and self-absorption. Their personal pain and shame caused them to become defensive and protective of their own interests and to develop the tendency to blame, exploit, and dominate one another. The harder they seemed to try to maintain a sense of intimacy and "oneness," the more they seemed to have been frustrated and disappointed. Creating "connectedness" became a complex and difficult task.

In her pain and brokenness, Eve developed a fervent and insatiable desire to control her husband by using her feminine charm, cunning, and manipulation. Genesis 3:16 (NIV) says that Eve was told, "your desire will be for your husband." This was not to suggest that she would simply seek to please or pleasure him. Rather, the Hebrew word for "desire" (*teshuqah*) is neither a pleasant nor a romantic word. *Teshuqah* means to have an insatiable desire to control another person (cf. Genesis 4:6, 7).[29] And to achieve this,

Eve would become like the serpent who used his cunning, sly, and crafty ways to accomplish his objective and elicit support for his wounded pride and revengeful spirit.

Adam reciprocated to this changed relationship in similar ways. He blamed Eve for his miserable self-loathing and sought to dominate and control her by ruling over her in the relationship (Genesis 3:16). By acting with supremacy and seeking to take control of the situation, Adam acted toward Eve with the same air of arrogance and superiority he had shown toward God. He even attacked God's character by suggesting that it was His fault because "the woman *You* put here with me"—she enticed me into disobedience (Genesis 3:12, NIV).

This fall from grace certainly compromised God's intentions for marriage. As Adam and Eve struggled to maintain connection and commitment to one another, the pain of their distrust and disloyalty served only further to wound them and their relationship. Their sense of personhood and equality was ruptured, and they began to feel the pain of invalidation and inequality. Deprived of commitment to one another, their sexuality, which had been such a wonderful vehicle for the establishment of intimacy and bonds of affection, now failed to enchant them or enhance their sense of meaning and spirituality in the same way. How quickly sexuality, when deprived of commitment, can become selfish and impersonal and degenerate into superficiality, abusiveness, and boredom.[30] Their search for intimacy and a recapturing of that sense of oneness that they had originally embraced had become illusionary. As a result, these changes have had a sad and tragic effect on marriage, which can be seen in the alienation, unfaithfulness, neglect, abuse, violence, dominance, desertion, separation, divorce, and sexual perversions that so often have characterized love relationships down through the centuries until this day.

The Redemption of Marriage

The curse of Genesis 3 is not God's final word regarding marriage. While sin may have perverted God's ideal for marriage, His grace precedes such destruction and bareness. The ingredients of the covenant relationship existed as a presupposition to the creation account. Those created in the image of God are, through the revelation of the good news about God, to be restored to His likeness. Grace means the recovery of a relationship with the living God and reconciliation in relationship with each other.[31] It confronts the conflict, competition, and punitive behaviors of broken relationships by declaring that God seeks to restore marriage to its original ideal through oneness, equality, and mutuality made possible through Jesus Christ. In Him, God seeks to restore to wholeness all those who have failed to attain the divine ideal in marriage.

In numerous ways throughout human history, God has called for the restoration of marriage to its purity and beauty. The prophets exalted marriage by using it to describe God's love (Isaiah 54:5, 6), and they decried the abuses that befell the marriage relationship.[32] The wisdom literature celebrates the romance and friendship as well as the covenant faithfulness that exist between a husband and wife. Proverbs 5:15-20.

The Song of Songs highlights this "return to Eden" theme in a number of significant ways. First, the names of both the lovers (Shulamite and Solomon) in the story are variations of the Hebrew word *shalom* ("peace" or "completeness"), indicating the epitome of intimacy and oneness. Second, the repetition of the miniature marriage covenant formula, "My lover is mine and I am his" (Song of Songs 2:16; 6:3, NIV) supports the ideas of friendship, individuality, belonging, and freedom of choice, and highlights the way in which both lovers invite each other to intimacy. Here they do not control or exert power over one another; instead, they freely give themselves to each other and to the marriage relationship. And third, the expression "I belong to my lover and his desire is for me" (Song of Songs 7:10) should be seen as a restoration of the balance of desire (*teshuqah*) distorted by the curse of Genesis 3:16.[33]

In the New Testament era, the Gospels depicted Jesus as approving marriage and challenging the evils that had caused division and separateness between the sexes. Through the symbolism contained in the supernatural transformation of water into wine at the wedding feast of Cana, Jesus demonstrated that the old ways were to be replaced by a new, refreshing, vitalizing power found only in Him. John 2:1-10. Clearly, Jesus supported the views about marriage expressed in Genesis 1 and 2, not the changed view of marriage that emerges from Genesis 3. (See Matthew 19:4-6.) He indicated that His followers were not to use their power and authority to coerce or control others (Matthew 20:25, 26) but instead were to adopt new and loving ways of relating to one another.

Jesus also consciously sought to restore the gender balance and erase the inequalities that existed between the sexes. With graciousness and sensitivity, He sought to lift women up from their inferior status. "He treated women as people...[and] went out of His way to refute by His actions the attitudes toward women,"[34] or, as John Stott says, "without any fuss or publicity, Jesus terminated the curse of the fall, reinvested woman with her partially lost nobility, and reclaimed for his new kingdom community the original creation blessing of sexual equality."[35]

The apostle Paul admonished the early church to "honour marriage and guard the sacredness of sexual intimacy between husband and wife" (Hebrews 13:4, *THE MESSAGE*). He, too, clearly upheld the Genesis 2:24 view of marriage and believed that the curse of Genesis 3, which involved the subjection of the wife to the husband, was neutralized and reversed by the love and service emphasized in the gospel concept of mutual submission. Ephesians 5:21-30. This mutual submission is demonstrated by spouses who care, honor, nurture, cherish, and love one another with self-sacrificing love. The apostle Peter also suggests a reversal of the curse by saying that husbands and wives who embrace the redemptive power of Christ's love become "heirs together of the grace of life" (1 Peter 3:7).

Strengthening Marriages

The Christian message clearly reveals that God is invested in restoring to wholeness all who fall short of His glorious ideals. It declares that He seeks to restore marriage to its original ideal through the oneness, equality, and mutuality made possible through Jesus Christ. He gives us the assurance that as we stretch toward those ideals, He will empower us to grow and develop the attitudes, skills, and behaviors necessary to experience the security and joy of a meaningful relationship.

The church today is called to uphold God's ideal for marriage and at the same time, be a reconciling, forgiving, healing community that shows understanding and compassion when brokenness occurs. Just as Moses in the Old Testament and Paul in the Christian era struggled with problems caused by broken marriages (Deuteronomy 24:1-5, 1 Corinthians 7:10-16), so the church must seek to strengthen marriages by working constructively and redemptively with those who fall short of the divine standard. It must be committed to encouraging marital partners to realize more and more the personal and relational potential inherent in their relationship. In this way, a couple's experience through marriage may become a conscious or an unconscious search for healing and wholeness Throughout the marital journey, a couple forms affectional ties and bonds that have the capacity to create an identification and connection with a marital partner—an "empathic other," or a covenantal God, who leads and empowers them toward growth and healing.

Through a variety of ministries, the church can assist couples to prepare for marriage by helping them explore a broad range of relational issues. It can also help married couples enrich their relationship by developing the skills and behaviors that lead to a greater sense of intimacy and enjoyment and that lead to achieving God's design for marriage. The church must also be more intentional about encouraging individuals in marital crisis to resolve their differences and build healthy marriages. It needs to provide couples with spiritual nurture and emotional support and take appropriate steps to protect those who are vulnerable to violence and abusive behaviour in their relationship.

Notes:

1. Warwick Hartin, *Why Did I Marry You?* (Melbourne: Hill of Content, 1998), p. 2.

2. Ibid., p. 8.

3. Ray Anderson, *Everything That Makes Me Happy I Learned When I Grew Up* (Illinois: Intervarsity Press, 1995), p. 166.

4. See Deuteronomy 28:20; Judges 10:13; 2 Chronicles 34:15; Isaiah 1:4.

5. Samuel Terrien, *Till the Heart Sings: Biblical Theology of Manhood and Womanhood* (Philadelphia: Fortress Press, 1985), pp. 14, 15.

6. Earl S. Kalland, *Theological Wordbook of the Old Testament,* vol. 3 (Chicago: Moody Press, 1981), pp. 177, 178.

7. Ibid., p. 15.

8. See Deuteronomy 10:12; 11:22; 13:4; Joshua 22:5; 23:8.

9. Raymond Collins, *The Bible and Sexuality* (Biblical Theological Bulletin, vol. 7, 1977), p. 153.

10. Markus Barth, *Ephesians* (New York, 1974), quoted in Leon Morris, *Reflections on the Letter to the Ephesians* (Michigan: Baker Books, 1994), p. 184.

11. John N. Oswalt, *Theological Wordbook of the Old Testament,* vol. 1 (Chicago: Moody Press, 1981), p. 136.

12. Otto A. Piper, *The Biblical View of Sex and Marriage* (New York: Charles Scribner & Sons, 1960), p. 28.

13. Ibid., p. 25.

14. Samuel Terrien, *Till the Heart Sings*, pp. 15, 16.

15. John Herbert and Fern Miles, *Husband-Wife Equality* (New Jersey: Fleming Revell, 1978), p. 164.

16. Samuel Terrien, *Till the Heart Sings*, p. 15.

17. John Temple Bristow, *Love, Marriage and Family* (St Louis: Chalice Press, 1994), pp. 82-86.

18. Ibid., p. 84.

19. Ibid., p. 72.

20. Ibid., p. 72.

21. Ibid., pp. 87-89.

22. Ibid., p. 71.

23. Walter Brueggemann, *Catholic Biblical Quarterly* 32:535, 1970.

24. Geoffrey Robinson, *Covenant and Commitment*, unpublished paper presented at Charles Sturt University, May, 1998.

25. Ibid.

26. See Proverbs 2:17; Jeremiah 31:31-34; Ezekiel 11:20; 14:11; Zechariah 8:8; Malachi 2:14.

27. Loren Wade, *Marriage and Covenant*, unpublished paper, Montemorelos University, Mexico, 1998.

28. Ray Anderson, *The Soul of Ministry* (Louisville: Westminister John Knox Press, 1997), p. 39.

29. John Temple Bristow, *Love, Marriage and Family*, pp. 67, 68.

30. Eugene H. Petersen, *Subversive Spirituality* (Vancouver: Regent College Publishing, 1997), p. 38.

31. Ray Anderson, *The Soul of Ministry*, pp. 52-59.

32. See 2 Samuel 12:1-9; Ezekial 22:9-11; Malachi 2:16.

33. Ron and Karen Flowers, *Love Aflame* (Hagerstown, Md.: Review and Herald Publishing Association, 1992), pp. 81-86.

34. Patricia Gundy, *Heirs Together* (Grand Rapids: Zondervan Publishing House, 1980), p. 46.

35. John Stott, *Involvement: Social and Sexual Relationships in the Modern World* (Old Tappan: Fleming H. Revell Company, 1984), p. 136.

TWO

The Quest for Intimacy in Marriage

It was a most extraordinary event. The funeral of Diana, Princess of Wales, on September 6, 1997 evoked such a public outpouring of grief that some journalists and commentators referred to it as a "special moment in history, after which nothing will ever be the same again." The worldwide telecast of the funeral was in fact the biggest live outside broadcast the BBC has ever made, shown in 187 countries and heard in forty-four languages by nearly two and half billion people. Outside the gates of the royal residences at Kensington and Buckingham Palaces, a vast field of sixty million flowers was placed in honor of the Princess who called herself "the Queen of Hearts." Obviously, many people had been "touched by the magic" of Diana's life and service, and even the most cynical observers were bewildered and surprised by their own tears.

The Queen said that there were lessons to be found in Diana's life. Certainly, her life was full of paradoxes. Her fairy-tale courtship and marriage to the Crown Prince of England had ended in acrimony and divorce. She was embraced by an adoring public, only to be discarded by the palace. She dazzled the world with her radiant beauty, yet she had to work hard at looking good. She was a dynamic and compassionate spokesperson, yet she struggled for acceptance and credibility. She made love a priority, yet she sacrificed her own self-esteem along the way. Carol Gilligan, Professor of Gender Studies at Harvard University, said that most women felt a strong sense of connectedness with Diana.[1] She was rejected, unloved, and alone, yet she groped for a way of life that would end her isolation and shame and reconnect her with others. She had become an icon of emotional need, befitting our time.

Searching for Love and Intimacy in a Post-Modern World

Commenting on the phenomenal outpouring of emotion that Diana's tragic death evoked, John Gray, Professor of Politics at Oxford University, said in *The Express* newspaper the following day that "the funeral was a mirror in which the nation saw clearly for the first time how profoundly it has changed" and how it had "opened up the spiritual vacuum in the hearts of post-modern people." In reflecting on how Britain had changed, he spoke of the massive cultural shift that has occurred in the western world, which has seen society move from modernist ideals to post-modern values. This emerging culture elevates feelings above reason; prizes intimacy, self-realization and personal loyalties over traditional social conventions; and places personal fulfilment before the preservation of any relationship in which the need for intimacy is frustrated. It is a culture that values emotional vulnerability yet finds it hard to agree on what constitutes our own ultimate good.

The events surrounding the life and death of Diana certainly highlighted for all of us the extent to which this shift in values has occurred in recent decades. After a century of triumphant technology, economic growth, and social reform, we have all become a lot more independent, self-sufficient, and pragmatic. Disenchanted with dogma and authority, we have dispensed with the old boundaries and social institutions. Marriage, family, and community life have broken down, and the Christian values that have undergirded public morality have lost their appeal and credibility. There is no such thing as absolute truth. All truth is relative and individually constructed. Gone is our past obsession with rationality, reason, and progress, as now we embrace diversity, difference, and plurality.

Brian Carrell argues that the emergence of post-modernity is really only modernity coming to understand itself more fully. He describes how post-modern thinking that elevates individual and personal rights has come at a considerably cost to community, social responsibility, and family life. A relentless pursuit of greater personal freedom has only resulted in social alienation, loneliness, and a lawlessness that arises from having no purpose, meaning, or direction in life. Furthermore, the narcissistic preoccupation with "the self," which gives birth to a sense of entitlement, is an obsession that goes way beyond any search for authenticity.[2]

Carrell further suggests that the unprincipled pragmatism of postmodernity has produced a growing sense of confusion and fragmentation. All the master stories in the narratives of the past have been rejected (e.g.: the biblical account of origins, the economic analysis of Marx, and Freud's psychological development of the psyche), and what has emerged is an emphasis on superficiality and the need to experience "the moment"—the perpetual present that allows for no sense of memory or historical continuity. The past has little value and the future little hope.[3]

Perhaps the existential grief experienced by so many at the time of Diana's death underscores just how much we feel the loss of meaning and purpose in our lives and how much we long for the certainty and hope that comes from being connected to others in community. Without being able to articulate the reasons for our pain, we feel the superficiality and rootlessness of our existence. Is it possible that we have lost the art of being caring and compassionate? Has the ability to enjoy intimacy and closeness begun to elude us?

Our search for love and intimacy has always been influenced by our social context and carried out against the backdrop of the culture in which we live. The rapidly changing social and economic conditions of the past few decades have definitely changed our expectations of marriage and the nature of human relationships. As mentioned in the previous chapter, marriage has shifted from being an institution that provides stability and security in the struggle for survival, to being a relationship or partnership built on companionship and emotional intensity.[4]

The most profound change in our expectations about marriage has come as a result of the gender revolution which has grown out of changes in the status of women. Don Edgar described the heart of this revolution when he said, "The breaking of the inherent link between sex and reproduction," with the commercialization of the contraceptive pill and the rise of the feminist movement in the 1960s, freed "both men and women from being locked into the old gender power dance"[5] and gave women, in particular, the opportunity to rethink their self concepts and envision a future not previously conceived or experienced. Increasingly, "the combination of sexual autonomy, higher education, workforce involvement, a secular attitude, and new concepts of partnerships and gender equality have transformed the bargaining base on which many contemporary women view the prospect of marriage."[6]

With these changes for women, men have also been challenged to act and respond in new ways. They have been required to develop new patterns of partnering in order to connect with women who are more informed, articulate, and sexually literate. The new partnership mode of marriage that many couples now aspire to achieve places a strong emphasis on the need for effective relational skills and a greater adaptability as they face each other with a new sense of honesty and openness. However, this egalitarian style of marriage tends to be more vulnerable to divorce because people expect so much more from it, making it more precarious and fragile.[7]

Is it any wonder that forming and maintaining quality relationships has become the number one social issue today? Is it surprising that our search for love and intimacy in marriage has become so confusing and frustrating? Helping people to connect in a disconnected world is a challenging task indeed. When people are unclear or uncertain about the script for marriage, it always makes intimacy more difficult to achieve. Because of this, we are confronted with the need to generate a clearer understanding of what we mean by "love" or "being in love." We need to explain more fully what processes generate intimacy in marriage and how to develop a quality, long-term relationship.

If the Christian church wants to seize the present opportunity to reach out to individuals and couples within its communities, it will need to give a very clear message about relationships and how to establish secure, stable marriages in ways that make sense to the post-modern mind. In developing its approach to educating couples about the nature and dynamics of marriage, the church needs to incorporate the following strategies:

1. Use an approach to educating couples that is simple, direct, and pragmatic. It will need to show them how to make their marriage work. Most couples are goal oriented and want to know how to preserve their relationship.

2. Present an optimistic view of relationships and marriage that instills hope and confidence for the future.

3. Use the current emphasis on emotion and feelings to show how these do not supplant the guiding hand of reason but constitute the dynamic heart of marriage.

4. Shift the focus from "the individual" and show how meaning, acceptance, and values are most powerfully found and reinforced through kinship and community— the place where cohesion, mutual support, and the bonds of love, commitment, and responsibility are forged and held together.

5. Affirm the importance of the "autonomy of self" and show how marriage requires a balance between separateness and connectedness.

6. Enable couples to hear each other's story through showing respect, empathy, admiration, trust, and affection and by creating a joint narrative that is embedded in emotional connectedness with others in community and a living connection with historic biblical traditions.

7. Recognize that post-modern couples are open to the spiri-

tual dimensions of life, and rather than ignoring this aspect of our humanity, seek to show the relevance of those master stories that make sense and are verifiable with scientific investigation.

8. Create a realistic view of the world that resists the desire to collapse the past and the future into the present and live only "in the moment."

9. Expose the culture of consumerism that sees truth, meaning, and knowledge as consumer items and that produces a personality that is shallow, self-absorbed, suspicious of commitment and attachment, frequently incapable of loyalty, and dedicated to keeping all options open. This self-contained ethic needs to be addressed if emotional connections are to be made.

What Is This Thing Called Love?

In our attempt to minister to couples in this changing social context, what can we do to help them develop a sense of closeness and togetherness? Current expectations about marriage emphasize the quality of the relationship and stress the need for couples to be successful in making their egalitarian partnership work. So what information and practical guidance can we give on how to establish and maintain a companionate marital relationship that will be both instructional and motivational? Without question, the key to the quality and viability of this companionate relationship is love—a love that is both romantic and passionate, nurturing and satisfying.

The problem is that the word *love* itself is one of the most misused and misunderstood words in our language. Trying to define what love is has always presented some difficulties. It is seen as one of the world's great mysteries. Even wise King Solomon once said that one of the things that was too wonderful and too amazing for him to understand was "how a man loves a woman" (Proverbs 30:19, NLT).

Furthermore, there are many myths or irrational beliefs about love that prevent us from coming to an adequate understanding of what genuine love really is. We tend to create and maintain these irrational beliefs that interfere with our intimate relationships and happiness. Most of the myths are perpetuated by storytellers in novels, movies, and television and suggest that love is matter of chemistry and is associated with intense passion, an overwhelming sense of romantic love, and a preoccupation based on fantasy that believes in instantaneous connection with another.

These notions of "romantic love" so prevalent in our present society have their genesis in the popular literature and events of the late Middle Ages in Europe. This literature immortalized gallant men who risked everything to serve or save the women they loved. It created heroes out of those young couples who defied the arranged marriage plans of their parents and sacrificed all in order to marry for love. This romanticized ideal, which had been relatively unknown in marriage up until this time, became the basis on which couples sought to voluntarily enter marriage.

As a result, romantic love soon came to be highly prized as a value that expressed the passionate attachment between two people who were not only emotionally involved but sexually attracted to each other. This understanding led people to view love as a delightful passion and a priceless emotional gift capable of generating the most profound ecstasy. In our present society, which fiercely prizes individualism, personal freedom, and individual choice, it is not hard to see why romantic love is so deeply rooted in our conscious pursuit of happiness.

Our understanding of love tends to be sabotaged by the following three myths:

1. Love is blind. This belief suggests that a person who "falls in love" simply accepts the other person without any conscious awareness or cognitive acknowledgement of their weaknesses, differences, or shortcomings.

2. Love is external. In other words, love is beyond our control. It is not a feeling generated from within. We are simply victims of fate and the external forces of love that are so mysterious, intense, and volatile they just "come over" us. "Being in love" does not require a decision on our part, because love just "hits you" unexpectedly—it is your destiny.

3. Love is uncontrollable. "Falling in love," being "swept off your feet," or being "head over heels in love," is an experience that can strike you at any time when you least expect it. It is intense and short-lived and pursues its own course. It comes as rapid, momentary surges of emotion, and you must go with it or you may lose it. There is no suggestion that you might or can nurture this love or indeed accept any responsibility for its presence or growth.

The fact that we cannot agree on a definition of what love is only serves to highlight that love is different things to different people. We use the word *love* to describe everything from a hypnotic emotional response to a zero score in tennis. It is associated with feelings of attraction, infatuation, sexual arousal, affection, and admiration. We have the great ability to simplify our lives by repeating the sentiments of the Beatles' song that says, "All you need is love, love...that is all you need," yet we have no precise idea of what is it that we have when we have got it or what it is that we aspire to experience. So perhaps a significant starting point in our journey to find intimacy in marriage would be first to define what love is and how it manifests itself in healthy stable marriages.

Many social scientists have attempted to define, measure, and describe various conceptions of what love is. However, Nathaniel Branden warns us that first we need to be sure we know what kind of love we are talking about, because "there are different kinds of love that can unite one human being to another. There is love between parents and children. There is love between siblings. There is love between friends. There is a love made of caring and affection but devoid of sexual feelings. And there is the kind of love we call "romantic love." He goes on to suggest that when we do speak of love, we are describing "our emotional response to that which we value highly" and that "to love another human being is to know and be known by them." Love is, he says "the experience of joy in the existence of the loved object, joy in proximity, and joy in interaction or involvement."[9]

Luciano L'Abate defines love as "the importance we attribute to ourselves and to others," evidenced by our ability "to share joys, hurts or fears of being hurt." The result of such sharing, he believes, is the development of a committed, close, and prolonged relationship."[10] Bernard Murstein, who has been studying the nature of love for the past three decades, says that love involves "a host of characteristics such as altruism, intimacy, admiration, respect, sharing, confiding, acceptance, pride in the other, unity and exclusive preoccupation," but that each of these characteristics "can be classified by mode of expression as a behaviour, a judgement or a feeling."[11]

These comments are extremely helpful and underscore a very important distinction in the way we define and understand what love is. Murstein's suggestion is that love is not just a feeling of the heart, a decision of the mind, or a behavioural response—it involves all three modes of expression. This is in contrast to the views expressed by so many people over the years that love is a feeling—a passionate, irrational feeling—or that love is a principle, a decision of the rational mind. What Murstein is stressing here is the multidimensional way that love is manifest in human experience.

Professor Pat Noller from the University of Queensland agrees. She believes that love is best understood as an attitude we adopt toward a particular person and that this "love" has three components:

1. A Cognitive component—*attitudes* about oneself and others, a *decision* to commit oneself to the loved one, and *beliefs* and *expectations* about love that come from our culture.

2. An Emotional component—*feelings* of warm enjoyment, of companionship, highly sexualized passionate feelings, and other feelings such as admiration, respect, and caring.

3. A Behavioral component—where love is revealed in *tangible actions* that express love toward another. These loving actions will be influenced by one's gender, personality, and beliefs about what love is and what are the appropriate ways of expressing it.

Furthermore, she suggests that "the way these three aspects of love are manifest in each individual will determine whether an experience of love involves a stable, healthy growth-producing relationship or an immature, overdependent and growth-stifling relationship."[12] She further asserts that the emotional and behavioral aspects of love are both strongly affected by the ideas and cognitions about love that are prevalent in the culture which we embrace.[13]

A model of love that integrates many of our ideas and concepts about love is contained in the work of Robert Sternberg from Yale University. His significant research about what we actually mean when we talk about "love" is simply expressed in a triangular theory of love, which focuses on clusters of factors involved in our expressions of love. His theory suggests that building a mature, complete, or consummate love relationship involves three active components that are balanced but vary in intensity over time. The three components of love, according to this theory, are:

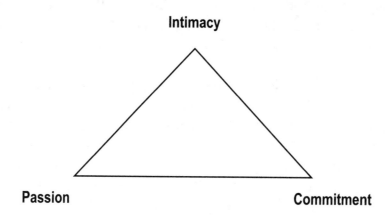

Figure 1: Sternberg's Model of Love

1. Passion is a component that refers to the drives that lead to romance, physical attraction, and sexual consummation in a loving relationship. It involves sexual desire and attraction and an intense longing for union with the other person. Sternberg states that although sexual needs may form the major part of passion in many relationships, there are other needs such as self esteem, affiliation with others, dominance over others, submission to others, and self-actualization which may constitute the component of passion in relationships.

2. Intimacy refers to the feelings of closeness, connectedness, and bonding that individuals may experience in a love relationship. It includes those feelings that create the experience of warmth, respect, and concern. In fact, Sternberg identified the following ten signs of intimacy which he considers to exist in all love relationships:

a. Desiring to promote the welfare of the loved one.

b. Experiencing happiness with the loved one.

c. Having high regard for the loved one.

d. Being able to count on the loved one in times of need.

e. Mutual understanding with the loved one.

f. Sharing one's self and one's possessions with the loved one.

g. Receiving emotional support from the loved one.

h. Giving emotional support to the loved one.

i. Having intimate communication with the loved one.

j. Valuing the loved one in one's life.

3. Commitment, the decision/commitment component of love, consists of two aspects: (a) The *decision* that one makes to love someone, and (b) the *commitment* one makes to maintain that love through good and bad times.[14] Sternberg's model is also helpful in that it differentiates between eight possible types of love generated by the triangular theory. He shows that where love is deficient in any of the three components of passion, intimacy, and commitment, it can be seen as less than mature, complete, or consummate—and in some cases, as immature.

Sternberg classifies and represents the different kinds of love as subsets of these three components in the following ways:

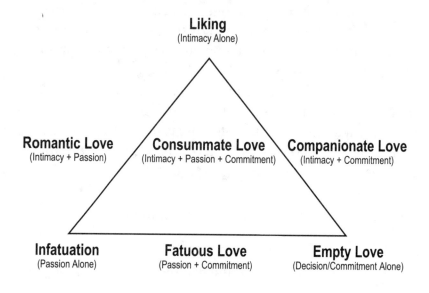

Figure 2: Sternberg's Eight Types of Love (Non-Love Being the Eighth)

Liking refers to the set of feelings and experiences in relationships that are true friendships, in which an individual feels closeness, bondedness, and warmth toward the other, without intense passion or long-term commitment.

Infatuated Love is "love at first sight," or the love that turns toward obsession, with the partner being loved as an idealized object rather than as him or herself. It results from passionate arousal in the absence of the intimacy and commitment components of love. It can arise and dissipate quickly and is characterized by a high degree of mental and physical arousal.

Empty Love is often found in stagnant relationships that have lost the mutual emotional involvement and physical attraction that once characterized them—relationships in which there is commitment but no intimacy or passion.

Romantic Love is where two lovers are drawn to one another both physically and emotionally but demonstrate no sense of commitment to each other. They may feel passionate toward one another and feel that they can bare their souls to each other, but realize that permanence in the relationship is unlikely, impossible, or simply an issue to be dealt with at some future time.

Companionate Love results from a combination of intimacy and commitment in a relationship in which physical attraction (as a major source of passion) has waned.

Fatuous Love is the type of love that is high on passion and commitment but low on intimacy and lacks the stabilizing element of intimate involvement. Sternberg describes this love as the kind of love we sometimes associate with Hollywood or with whirlwind courtships.

Non-Love is simply the absence of all three components of love.

Consummate or Complete Love results when all three components are present. It is the kind of love toward which many of us strive, especially in romantic relationships. Attaining it can be difficult, but keeping it is even harder. This constitutes a mature love experience—a love we want to make as complete as possible.[15]

Sternberg further presents a "developmental" view of the three components of love, suggesting that passion, intimacy, and commitment do change over time as they move toward or away from the creation of love relationships based on mutual understanding and interdependency. He represents the completely balanced relationship by an equilateral triangle and suggests that issues such as the idealization of one's partner by another, the level of satisfaction experienced in the love relationship, and the perceptions developed by each person about their love for the other person can be influenced by individual values and beliefs, personality differences, and levels of adaptability. He also shows how these things can influence the intensity and future of the relationship.

Another fascinating and relevant aspect of the triangular theory of love is the way in which Sternberg incorporates the notion that love involves aspects that are cognitive, emotional, and behavioral in nature. He has developed the concept of an "action triangle" that represents the various ways in which the three components of love (which represent more cognitive and affective aspects of love) are translated in actions (behaviors).

▶ Actions that indicate *passion* are expressed through touching, hugging, kissing, and making love.

▶ Actions that give expression to *intimacy* include communicating inner feelings, offering emotional and material support, and expressing empathy for the other.

▶ Actions that express *commitment* may include such things as expressing fidelity, staying in a relationship through tough times, or giving some tangible symbol like a ring to the other person.

The overall strength of the triangular model of love is that it provides a dynamic view of what makes love relationships work and offers a simple diagnostic measure that is helpful in those settings where couples desire a greater sense of connectedness and intimacy. It also enables them to move more easily from a cognitive understanding of the components involved in love to generating those behavioral changes that will create a greater affective involvement and maintain their relationship through good and tough times.

The Commitment Component

The commitment component in Sternberg's theory has received some additional interesting elaborations through the work of George Levinger and Scott Stanley. The current phenomena of "commitment phobia" that manifests itself in many post-modern love relationships has generated a great degree of interest among researchers wishing to understand the importance that commitment plays in the creation of a stable, mature love relationship. For Sternberg, the commitment component determines the stability and maintenance of the relationship and involves two aspects: a *decision* to love a certain other and a *commitment* to maintain that love.

Levinger, in analyzing marital cohesiveness, found that the commitment-related aspects of the marital bond grew out of two distinctly separate sources, one internally driven, the other externally generated. He discovered that the decision to make a commitment to the relationship was driven by a sense of internally experienced obligations and by a sense of externally generated constraints around marriage.[16]

This work is further extended in the current research being carried out by Scott Stanley at the University of Denver. He has developed a model of commitment that features two elements—dedication and constraint.

Dedication is evidenced by a desire (and associated behaviors) not only to continue in the relationship but also to improve it, sacrifice for it, protect it, invest in it, and seek the other's welfare, not simply one's own. These six desires are closely associated with an internally motivated decision to commit to the marriage relationship. Stanley found that dedication is strongly associated with the quality of the marriage and is something that the individual has a choice about, namely, how much of themselves they are going to give to their spouse.

Constraint refers to forces that constrain an individual to maintain a relationship regardless of their personal feelings about it. It involves a sense of obligation toward the other person and the relationship in which they are both involved. There are certain constraints that favor relationship stability by making the termination of the relationship more economically, socially, personally, and psychologically costly.

For Stanley, constraint is what gives stability and a sense of security in a marriage. Without "constraint commitment," he believes that it is possible that no marriage would stay together, because no marriage is consistently satisfying. His research shows that constraint grows over time and changes in marriage. It really is evidence of choices that have been made from dedication in the past. Constraint leads individuals to make more constructive choices in marriage during times of trauma and crisis. When it is all boiled down, commitment in all of its complexity leads to a long-term view in a marriage. This is vital to a marriage, because it enables two people to see beyond the ups and downs of relational life and make an investment in the marriage for the long haul.[17]

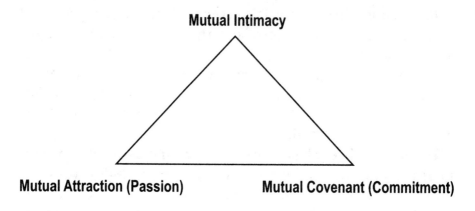

Figure 3: Aspects of Love That Sustain Marriage

These concepts of love and marriage, and the components of love expressed so simply by Sternberg in his triangular theory of love, bear a remarkable similarity to the emphasis given by the Creator-God at the beginning of human history. The Bible clearly states that God instituted marriage based on a partnership sustained by love and companionship (Genesis 2:18, 24) and that this relationship was characterized by its oneness or sense of mutual intimacy (intimacy) that grew out of mutual attraction (passion) and a covenantal relationship (commitment). These factors were designed to keep the relationship stable over time through an ongoing, quality interaction that deepens the emotional investment between these two marital partners.

Understanding Love As Attachment

Another important way of conceptualizing and understanding what love is and the part it plays in the development of an intimate love relationship can be seen through the emotional/cognitive process of human attachment or bonding. Our understanding of the bonding process grows out of Attachment theory, developed by John Bowlby. He believed that the process of attachment is the source and foundation of love and that emotional bonds develop primarily through an individual being physically close to another on a consistent basis.

Bowlby postulated that children in their infancy begin to develop ideas and beliefs (cognitive) about themselves and other people based on the kind of emotional attachments or connections they form with others. These mental models (which may involve both positive and negative views of themselves and others) are constructed on the basis of the availability and responsiveness of their primary caregivers and the quality of the interaction with them. He believed that any threat or disruption to this emotional bond results in anxiety, which triggers in the infant feelings of distress that function to draw the caregiver back and reestablishes the bond. When there is no connection with the attachment figure, there is usually protest, clinging, despair, and detachment.[18] He further believed that these "inner working" models, which are central components of personality, not only regulate a person's social behavior and feelings but vitally affect the way they go about engaging in love relationships and determine the level to which they are able to achieve a sense of security, emotional closeness, and self-confidence in intimate relationships.

Daniel Stern further developed Bowlby's concept of attachment by demonstrating that emotion plays a central role in driving the formation, maintenance, disruption, and renewal of these inner working models. He contended that moments of emotional connection or "affect attunement" between a child and its primary caregivers result in both of them recording a series of memories that form the basis of attachment and contribute to the development of their self-confidence and healthy self-esteem. These "moments of mutual creation," Stern says, "constitute the ties of attachment—the stuff of being with another person." The formation of such attachment, he concluded, "consists of the memories and mental models of what happens between you and that other person. How you feel with them. What they can make you experience that others cannot. What you can permit yourself to do or feel or think or wish or dare—only in their presence. What you can accomplish with their support."[19]

Mary Ainsworth and colleagues have identified three types of attachment styles and have shown how these remain fairly stable across time. They describe these three styles as:

1. Secure Attachment is a sense of security that develops in which infants perceive their caregivers to be reliable and trustworthy sources of protection. They are calm and develop emotional closeness when their caregivers are consistently *available* and *responsive* to their emotional needs.

2. Anxious/Ambivalent Attachment develops where infants do not seem confident about the availability or responsiveness of their caregivers and perceive them to be insensitive, intrusive, inconsistent, and constantly misreading the child's needs. The infant tends to intersperse proximity/contact seeking with angry, resistant behavior and is not easily comforted in moments of immediate or intense distress.

3. Avoidant Attachment is formed when the caregivers are rigid, rejecting, hostile, or averse to physical contact with the child. The child also tends to manifest behaviors that are rigid and compulsive, rebuffs invitations to closeness, and is less expressive of positive emotions.[20]

Table 1 (see page 60) illustrates the way in which the three styles of attachment are formed. Emphasis is also given to the emotional and behavioral responses that are generated as a result of the emotional connections made between the child and caregivers. The table also highlights how these responses impact the development of the self and the individual's capacity for maintaining intimate adult relationships.

The research of Bowlby and others has given us one of the simplest and most basic models for understanding how the emotional bonding process influences the development of love relationships in both childhood and adult life.

The work of Phillip Shaver, Cindy Hazan, and Donna Bradshaw in more recent years has illustrated how these three attachment styles account for the different behavior patterns people display in adult romantic love relationships. Attachment theory, they say, gives us a clue to the basis on which we feel loved and accepted and best illustrates how romantic pair-bonds are formed in adulthood.

Their studies have shown that **Secure** adults are comfortable giving and receiving love and reflect high levels of trust, affection, and intimacy. They have the ability to share ideas and feelings appropriately. Emotional and sexual intimacy comes naturally, and they feel that their romantic partner provides them with a sense of support, reassurance, connectedness, security, affection, and relief from distress.

Anxious/Ambivalent adults are described as "needy but angry." They exhibit a fear of not being loved sufficiently and have a need for constant reassurance. They tend to report high levels of obsessive preoccupation with their loved one. They often fall in love easily and have relationships characterized by intensity and chaos. They see their partner as unavailable and/or unresponsive.

Avoidant adults tend to deny the need for intimacy and have difficulty in trusting others and allowing emotional closeness. They are over-involved with work and other nonrelationship activities.[21] They can be highly sexual, having taken all their emotional and physical needs and channeled them into that one area.[22]

By using Hazan and Shaver's self-report measure [23] (see Table 2, page 62), couples and romantic partners can quickly identify from the simple descriptions of these three adult attachment styles their own style and feelings about close relationships and compare them with their partner's style of attachment. What is now quite clear from the research is that attachment styles in adults are important predictors of the quality of the marital relationship and are definitely related to the way couples interact, connect, and feel satisfied with their marriage.

Cohn and others found that couples containing at least one secure partner had more harmonious and less conflicted interactions then insecure couples. Couples in which both members were insecure experienced more conflict, produced less positive interactions, and functioned at a lower level than couples in which one or both members were secure. It seems likely that the presence of

Emotional Attachment based on Availability and Responsiveness of primary caregiver:

Are they Available?
Are they Responsive?

	▼	▼	▼
Perception of Caregiver	Yes	Sometimes	No
Emotional Response	Child feels Secure and Protected	Child feels Anxious and Insecure	Child feels Abandoned; Actively avoids Contact with Caregivers
Behavioral Response	Acts autonomously; Exploring behaviors encouraged	Constantly seeking Proximity/Closeness; Overactive; Attachment behaviors	Child switches off and avoids closeness; Things become more important; Pseudo-independent
Concept of Self	Fosters feelings of Confidence and Survival	Fosters feelings of Self-depreciation	Fosters feelings of Avoidance
Capacity for Loving Relationships	• Positive view of Self •Accepting and Adaptable •Comfortable with Closeness •Trusting and Affectionate	• Constantly needs Reassurance • Negative view of self •Blurred boundaries •High need for •Closeness and Intimacy driven by Anxiety	• Constantly feels Smothered • Negative view of self • Feels unacceptable of Intimacy from others * Distant and Discouraged • Avoids closeness

Table 1: The Development of Adult Styles of Attachment

one secure partner reduces the frequency of angry, hurtful, destructive interactions.[24]

Understanding How Intimacy Is Achieved

So far, we have explored a number of significant models that help us understand what love is. This discussion has been necessary background for our quest to discover and understand what intimacy is and how it is achieved in marriage. While it is possible that intimacy may be achieved for some couples through immediate emotional connection, it is not, generally speaking, an instantaneous process but a journey that takes years to develop. For some, intimacy may wax and wane, and it may never be fully realized. However, one thing is sure—there is no single or easy path to intimacy, and most do not achieve it without a struggle.[25] Bagarozzi says that intimacy is "a dynamic, interactive, and reciprocal process that evolves over time along with the development of a committed relationship. As the relationship grows and matures, intimacy deepens as self-awareness and self-disclosure increase."[26]

The word *intimacy* comes from the Latin word *intimus,* meaning "innermost." It refers to the unveiling of the "most deeply internal or inmost qualities of a person."[27] It involves two people who know each other and who intentionally disclose their thoughts and feelings to one another. They are open, honest, and affectionate toward each other; they have developed a special significance to one another; and they have a history of shared understanding and meaning. They recognize one another's weaknesses but choose to accept each other as equals and refuse to exert power or control over one another when resolving their differences.

L'Abate has proposed an interesting definition of love and intimacy. He relates the ability to love and to be intimate with the attribution of importance and the ability to share joys, hurts, or fears of being hurt. Exercising this ability is what develops emotional connections and personal closeness between two people and leads to a close, committed, long-term relationship. According to his research, intimacy is not particularly common in relationships, and most couples struggle to connect with each other's emotional experiences.

L'Abate clarifies our understanding of love and intimacy by suggesting that "intimacy becomes part of the sharing and self-disclosure of both pleasurable and painful experiences."[28] He says that the process of intimacy begins to develop as we make ourselves available and vulnerable to one another's hurts and pain by sharing with them their highs and the lows—laughing with them and crying with them. This, he says, is good for bonding and can

Style	Description
Secure	• I find it relatively easy to get close to others. • I am comfortable depending on others and having them depend on me. • I do not often worry about being abandoned or about someone getting too close to me. • I find it easy to trust others. • I feel confident about relating to others. I know they like and respect me.
Anxious/Ambivalent	• I find that others are reluctant to get as close as I would like. • I often worry that my partner does not really love me or won't want to stay with me. • I want to merge completely with another person, and this desire sometimes scares people away.
Avoidant	• I am somewhat uncomfortable being close to others. • I find it difficult to trust others completely—difficult to allow myself to depend on them. • I am nervous when anyone gets too close, and often, love partners want me to be more intimate than I feel comfortable being. • I am too busy with other activities to put time into relationships.

Table 2: Hazan and Saver's Description of the three Attachment Styles

be the ultimate demonstration that we understand, connect with, and share in their experience.

Furthermore, L'Abate contends that "the sharing of hurts also represents the ability to be separate and together simultaneously, because it requires the strength to join another in sharing hurt, while being separate enough to be available to the other without the demand for perfection, solutions, or performance."[29] He demonstrates through his studies on intimacy that "couples who do openly express their feelings of hurt, fear, and anger can have potent experiences of intimacy"[30] because it allows them to access the heart and soul of their partner. For L'Abate, hurt is the emotion basic to intimacy and close interpersonal relationships. It is the emotion that is common to all human existence, and it consists of the collection of all our painful experiences, traumatic losses, occasional or chronic failures, inevitable rejections, and the direct or indirect putdowns that we all experience in life.[31]

In summary, then, intimacy involves: (a) the importance we attribute to ourselves and others; the degree to which we are able to self-disclose and share in the intense emotional experiences (joys, hurts, and fears) of another, and (b) the ability to be emotionally available and join with another in their joys and pains without compromising our own personal boundaries and personhood. Of course, this presupposes that we have a secure sense of self and the ability to communicate effectively our thoughts and feelings, resolve our differences, and negotiate our way through conflict. Intimacy will obviously be inhibited if couples do not have the ability to listen with empathy, articulate their own inner experiences, and convey to the other person that they have heard, understood, and accepted their message.

Other obstacles to achieving intimacy may be centered in the different fears people may have about being shamed, abandoned, belittled, or engulfed by their partner or by the interactional processes of the relationship. The levels of intimacy experienced in a marriage are also influenced by the developmental and situational needs and concerns encountered throughout the various stages of the life cycle. As couples deal with the stresses and strains of life, these intimacy levels fluctuate considerably, especially during the child-rearing and middle years of marriage.

We also need to recognize that intimacy is experienced across the many different dimensions of a relationship. Schaefer and Olsen identify the following seven dimensions of marital intimacy:

1. **Emotional Intimacy**—the sharing of feelings, warmth, and desire.

2. **Social Intimacy**—the sharing of group experiences and common experiences of fun and play.

3. **Sexual Intimacy**—sharing a deep, personal closeness through sensual, erotic experiences and the experience of self-abandonment to another.

4. **Intellectual Intimacy**—the sharing of thoughts and ideas.

5. **Recreational Intimacy**—the sharing of leisure and recreational activities.

6. **Spiritual Intimacy**—the sharing of spiritual beliefs, values, and experiences.

7. **Aesthetic Intimacy**—sharing together the world of beauty and creativity.[32]

According to Hatfield, the experience of intimacy across all of these dimensions requires that we also acknowledge the way in which our intimate interactions are experienced and expressed. She suggests a model of intimacy that engages all three aspects of our personality—our thinking, feeling, and behavior. For her, these three aspects are:

Cognitive intimacy constitutes our willingness to comprehend the other person's story, to share profound information about each other, to make sense out of our self-disclosures, and to feel that we are truly and fully understood.

Emotional intimacy is about the way we express feelings of closeness and emotional bonding. It is reflected in our deep caring for one another, our ability to empathize and vicariously experience another's feelings, and our willingness to share the intense emotions generated within the relationship (such as tenderness, joy, love, hurt, and pain).

Behavioral intimacy refers to a partner's ability to seek out and enjoy close physical proximity and touch, the ability to effectively communicate both verbally and nonverbally in ways that affirm the private and personal nature of the relationship, and the ability to act with sensitivity and responsiveness.[33]

Qualities Essential for Sustaining Intimacy

Improving the level of intimacy in their relationship is seen by all couples as the primary goal of marriage. In our quest to understand what love is and how intimacy is achieved in marriage, we have explored a variety of factors that researchers say influence our relational satisfaction and happiness. Sternberg's model of love is most instructive in having us understand what we mean and expect when we talk about "being in love," and his three components of love—passion, commitment, and intimacy—highlight important components in the process of developing a satisfying, intimate relationship. Along with L'Abate's definition of intimacy that focuses on emotionally connecting with the joys, hurts, and fears of another person, we begin to see just how critical the emotional dimension is to building and maintaining a healthy marriage. In fact, Sternberg argues that while intimate relationships are bound to wax and wane in emotional intensity over time, it needs to be understood that intimacy is *primarily* an affective experience. It is the positive feelings of love, affection, and warmth that marriage partners express to each other that build intimacy and continually enhance the awareness that what transpires between them is healthy and desirable.[34]

For true intimacy to flourish in their relationship, a couple must be mutually invested in working at improving the quality of their interactions and seeking greater depths of understanding. Researchers suggest that there are three relational qualities necessary for sustaining intimacy in marriage.

1. Mutual trust and respect. Couples need to feel totally secure in sharing their innermost thoughts, feelings, beliefs, and values. They must be willing to trust and respect each other so that when they self-disclose to one another, they do not fear the possibility of being judged, evaluated, ridiculed, exploited, harmed, or betrayed. We know that intimacy never survives where there is no trust or respect.

2. Availability. Another important quality for intimate couples is the need to be emotionally available to each other, which means being willing to mutually share their hurts and joys. Being available means to be open to hearing and listening to your partner's pain—to empathize with them. It means being committed to the relationship and willing to spend time building and supporting a partnership that works and that is based on friendship and companionship.

3. Responsiveness. The third quality to sustaining intimacy involves a willingness on the part of couples to mutually share at similar levels of self-disclosure and self-revelation; to respond to each other with acceptance, affection, sensitivity, and understanding; to affirm common assumptions about the relationship; and to demonstrate the ability to stand back and reflect on feedback given about one's own style of communication and consider the possibility of changing how one relates. Being responsive also means being willing to deal with resentment and bitterness and to forgive and heal the hurts of the past.

By embracing these qualities, couples are most likely to experience satisfying levels of intimacy and achieve what Karen Prager describes as major benefits that occur in healthy and effectively functioning relationships. The three major benefits she lists are:

1. Stability—the feeling of partnership, solidarity, and persistence that avoids the prospect of distance, separation, or dissolution.

2. Satisfaction—evaluating the quality of the relationship as positive; feeling rewarded and fulfilled.

3. Harmony—the feeling that the relationship functions free of discord and that it is not constantly disrupted by cycles of chronic conflict or dysfunctional behavior.[36]

Couples who successfully bond with each other will have not only attained new levels of meaningful connection but will have discovered that love is not a thing or commodity to be purchased but a way of describing a relationship that is enjoyed. They will have discovered that intimacy is really about maximum closeness with a minimum of threat.

Perhaps the prayer of the apostle Paul for the Philippian believers is an appropriate prayer for all couples.

So this is my prayer: that your love will flourish and that you will not only love much but well. Learn to love appropriately. You need to use your **head** and test your *feelings* so that your love is sincere and intelligent, not sentimental [romantic] gush. Live a lover's life, circumspect and exemplary [*behavior*], a life Jesus will be proud of, bountiful in fruits from the soul, making Jesus Christ attractive to all, getting everyone involved in the glory and praise of God (Philippians 1:9-11, *THE MESSAGE*).

Notes:

1. Carol Gilligan, "For Many Women, Gazing at Diana Was Gazing Within," *The New York Times*, September 9, 1997.

2. Brian Carrell, *Moving Between the Times. Modernity and Postmodernity: A Christian View* (Auckland: The Deep Sight Trust, 1998), pp. 63-65.

3. Ibid., pp. 77-86.

4. Denis Ladbrook, *Social Context of Marriage and Family in Australia in the Mid to Late 1990s* (Australia: Prepare-Enrich, 1995), p. 22.

5. Donald Edgar, *Relationships in the New Millennium* (Deakin: Relationships Australia Incorporated, 1999), p. 42.

6. Denis Ladbrook, *Social Context of Marriage and Family in Australia in the Mid to Late 1990s* (Australia: Prepare), p. 16.

7. Ibid., pp. 6-15.

8. Brian Carrell, *Moving Between the Times*, pp. 81-90, 108-110, 114, 115.

9. Nathaniel Branden, "A Vision of Romantic Love," in the *Psychology of Love,* by Robert Sternberg and Michael Barnes, (New Haven: Yale University Press, 1988), pp. 219-222.

10. Jon Carlson and Len Sperry, *The Intimate Couple* (Philadelphia: Brunner/Mazel, 1999), p. 34.

11. Bernard L. Murstein, "A Taxonomy of Love," in the *Psychology of Love* by Robert Sternberg and Michael Barnes, (New Haven: Yale University Press, 1988), p. 26.

12. Patricia Noller, "What is this thing called Love?" in *Personal Relationships,* vol. 3, 1996, pp. 99, 100.

13. Ibid., pp. 111, 112.

14. Robert I. Sternberg, "Triangulating Love," in *Psychology of Love,* by Sternberg and Barnes, eds. (New Haven: Yale University Press, 1988), pp. 119-138.

15. Ibid., pp. 122-129.

16. George Levinger, "Can We Picture Love," in *Psychology of Love,* by Sternberg and Barnes, eds. (New Haven: Yale University Press, 1988), pp. 144, 145.

17. Scott Stanley, et al., *A Christian's Companion Guide to Fight for Your Marriage* (Denver: Christian PREP, Inc., 1996), pp. 24-26.

18. Jon Carlson and Len Sperry, *The Intimate Couple*, pp. 59, 60.

19. Jeri Doane and Diana Daimond, *Affect and Attachment in the Family* (New York: Basic Books, HarperCollins Publishers, 1994), p. 31.

20. Jack Dominian, *Marriage* (London: Heinemann, 1995), pp. 11-17.

21. Ibid., pp. 16, 17.

22. Jon Carlson and Len Sperry, *The Intimate Marriage*, pp. 61, 62.

23. Phillip Shaver, Cindy Hazan, and Donna Bradshaw, "Love As Attachment," in *Psychology of Love,* by Sternberg and Barnes, eds. (New Haven: Yale University Press, 1988), p. 80.

24. Robert J. Sternberg and Mahzad Hojjat, eds., *Satisfaction in Close Relationships* (New York: Guilford Press, 1997), pp. 42, 43.

25. Susan M. Johnson and Leslie Greenberg, *The Heart of the Matter* (New York: Brunner/Mazel, 1994), p. 121.

26. Dennis A. Bagarozzi, "Marital Intimacy," in *The Intimate Couple* by Jon Carlson and Len Sperry (Phildelphia: Brunner/Mazel, 1999), pp. 67, 81.

34 Ibid., pp. 53, 63.

35. Ibid., pp. 24, 25, 224.

36. Ibid., p. 219. Karen J. Prager, in *The Psychology of Intimacy* (New York: Guilford Press, 1995), p. 65.

37. Jon Carlson and Len Sperry, *The Intimate Couple*, p. 34.

38. Ibid.

39. Karen J. Prager, *The Psychology of Intimacy*, pp. 55, 56.

40. Susan M. Johnson and Leslie Greenberg, *The Heart of the Matter*, p. 116.

41. Jon Carlson and Len Sperry, *The Intimate Couple*, p. 66.

42. Karen Prager, *The Psychology of Intimacy*, pp. 47, 48.

THREE

Communication— the Key to Emotional Closeness

Being able to communicate is unquestionably the most important human survival skill. While nobody actually teaches us how to communicate effectively, the reality is that our whole existence depends on our ability to transfer information from ourselves to others and build relationships with those who can enrich our lives. As such, communicating with others is a wonderful gift, and it provides the key to understanding, friendship, and intimacy. Through the process of communication, we are able to give and receive love, express our thoughts and feelings to others, and acquire a knowledge and appreciation of others' needs and wishes.

The Bible writers speak of the powerful effect words can have in our relationships. They encourage us to "be gracious in our speech" and recognize that the goal of all communication should be "to bring out the best in others in conversation, not put them down, not cut them out" (Colossians 4:6, *THE MESSAGE*). The apostle Paul admonishes us to "speak the truth in love" (Ephesians 4:15, NIV) and recognize that honesty and openness in our relationships with one another is an important ingredient to making intimate connections. Proverbs 24:26, NIV. The wise man Solomon endorses the concept that "cutting words wound and maim but that kind words have the power to help and to heal" (Proverbs 15:4, *THE MESSAGE*).

Communication Is Vital to Relationship Satisfaction

Communication is a vital aspect of every marital relationship. After all, the marriage relationship is the product of a process of dialogue in which the ability to access and articulate feelings; resolve differences; and communicate personal ideas, beliefs, and values is very important to the couple.

Through the process of communication, marriage partners establish their own unique patterns of interacting with one another based on expressions, gestures, exchanges, and symbols. This interaction creates for them a relationship that either strives or thrives. Their idiomatic style of communicating forms a powerful emotional bond that establishes a strong sense of shared meaning and enjoyment.[1]

One of the most reliable research findings about intimate relationships is that "Communication is a primary determinant of relationship satisfaction"[2] and that the patterns of marital interaction constitute the key to predicting the quality of the marriage relationship.[3]

What we know is that the degree of positive regard that marital partners have for each other, the amount of interaction they share together, the effectiveness of their communication, and the level of emotional gratification they enjoy, all contribute toward their sense of fulfilment, stability, and satisfaction in the relationship.[4] This is why Emotionally Focused Marriage Education seeks to promote the growth and development of Emotionally Intelligent Marriages by focusing first and foremost on those aspects of the communication process between a couple that help them change and improve their relationship.

This approach is designed to facilitate their ability to: connect and dialogue with each other at the emotional level; access thoughts and feelings through appropriate self-revelation and self-disclosure; learn how to listen empathically and connect with the feelings and emotional experiences of their partner; and provide accurate playback and confirmation of the words and emotions expressed by their partner.

Aspects of Effective Communication

In order for couples to understand the dynamics involved in effective communication, they need to acknowledge the following six principles:

1. The skills of communication are learned. While most of us believe we are good at communicating, the reality is that we all need help to learn those skills that enable us to connect with others, especially at the emotional level. The process of building better relationships can be learned through developing the skills of self-awareness, self-disclosure, empathic listening, responding, and confirmation. Even though many of us have learned how to relate to others in reasonably effective ways through the process of attachment, few of us have not acquired a range of ineffective skills that grow out of our anxieties, uncertainties, or self-protectiveness.

2. It is impossible not to communicate. Pat Noller says that "It is impossible to not communicate! Many people do not understand this, because they limit their concept of communication to words and fail to realize that communication is going on whenever we are in the presence of someone else, even if we are only communicating that we want to have nothing to do with them."[5] We need to recognize that communication takes several forms—verbal, nonverbal and written—and that it occurs at three levels: the Content level—*what* is being shared; the Feeling level—*how you feel* about the content; how you relate to the message; and the Meaning level—the interpretation, significance, and value you attach to the message and your emotional response to its content.

3. How you feel about yourself affects how you communicate. Our ability to dialogue with others, listen to and connect with them, is strongly influenced by the level of our self-esteem. If our inner dialogue about ourselves is immersed in feelings of inferiority, inadequacy, or self pity, we become distracted and unfocused in our response to the communication that others make to us.

4. Empathic listening is a vital part of good communication. In most instances, it is not what you *say* that counts the most in the communication process but what others *hear* you say that matters. The art of listening and accurately receiving and interpreting the message is ultimately more significant than the sending of the message. As Stephen Covey says, "First seek to understand, then be understood."[6]

5. Playback before feedback. One of the cardinal rules of effective communication is that we always need to check out what we heard the other person say to make sure we are not making any incorrect assumptions about the message we have received. So often, our own biases or prejudices can cause us to make inaccurate or faulty interpretations.

6. Feelings are the essence of communication. It needs to be recognized that all communication involves the expression of emotion, either through the use of positive or negative feelings or through the intent or innuendo of language. One of the most critical factors in the communication process is the ability to identify and understand the feelings being expressed. Feelings are the gateway to a person's heart and soul. Connecting with another person's feelings constitutes the most powerful part of the intimacy process, because it brings with it a sense of closeness, vulnerability, and genuineness.

Frequently the emotional connection that does occur when two people connect at the feeling level is something that happens beyond the use of words. There is a synergy, a nonverbal connection, the creation of a moment of "affect attunement," as Daniel Stern would say. This ability to connect without any words being spoken is beautifully captured in the words of the song "When You Say Nothing at All," featured in the blockbuster movie "Notting Hill" and sung by Ronan Keating:

> *It's amazing how you can speak right to my heart*
> *Without saying a word, you light up the dark*
> *Try as I may, I can never explain*
> *What I hear when you don't say a thing.*

All day long I hear people talking about love
But when you hold me near, you drown out the crowd
Try as they may, they can never define
What's been said between your heart and mine.

The smile on your face lets me know that you need me
There's a truth in your eyes, saying you'll never leave me
The touch of your hand says you'll catch me whenever I fall
You say it best, when you say nothing at all.

These six principles are extremely helpful for couples to re-member, because they bring into focus issues at the core of all effective marital communication. And they highlight the need for marital partners to use and develop those skills and behaviors most critical in growing a strong, healthy relationship. Without a simple understanding of the ways good communication happens, couples will struggle and flounder to make connections and establish a sense of emotional closeness.

Levels of Communication

The freedom and comfort we feel in communicating is very much influenced by how safe and secure we feel about ourselves in the face of other people. The extent of our willingness to go out of ourselves and reveal our thoughts and feelings to others is de-scribed by John Powell in his book *Why Am I Afraid to Tell You Who I Am?*[7]

He suggests that there are five levels at which we communicate with others and that each level leads to greater depths of intimacy. Marital couples need to recognize the struggles associated with self-revelation and appreciate how they can negotiate their way through these five levels of communication (See Figure 4, next page).

Level Five: Cliché Conversation. This involves minimal self-disclosure. At this level we talk only in clichés, such as "How ya doing?" "What's up?" or "Good to see you." Such conversation is superficial and shares nothing of who we are or what we feel about

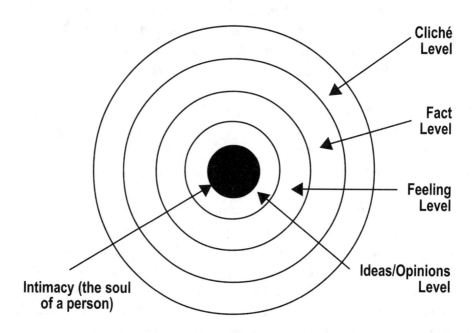

Figure 4: Five Levels of Communication

anything. In marriage, this level of dialogue only creates a lot of frustration, resentment, and distance.

Level Four: Reporting the facts about others. Here, there is still minimal self-disclosure. Just as we may hide behind clichés, so at this level, we seek to hide behind stories and narratives about other people. Content to pass on gossip about people and events in our world, we give nothing of ourselves and invite nothing from our partner in return.

Level Three: My ideas and opinions. Intimacy begins at this level of self-disclosure as we begin to share some of our own ideas and opinions with our partner. However, we are cautious and look for signs of acceptance as we risk sharing some of our ideas that reveal a little of our thoughts, decisions, or judgments. In expressing some of our own ideas, we give our partner some chance of getting to know us more intimately.

Level Two: My feelings and emotions. Communication at this level reveals a lot more about you and what goes on inside you.

Your feelings and emotions are what clearly differentiate you from others and tell your partner who you really are. At this level, genuine emotional honesty and openness occur, and intimate connections can take place.

Level One: Intimate communication. Authentic communion occurs at this level between two people who are willing to risk being absolutely open, honest, and genuine with each other. This personal encounter leads to deep insights and an authentic friendship that results from emotional connection, mutual empathy, and understanding.

The Process of Communication

Now let us turn our attention to the six stages of the communication process. By understanding the dynamics involved in the way two people connect with each other, a marital couple can be encouraged to understand how emotional attachments are formed and become motivated to take ownership of the six skills involved in effective communication.

1. Self-Awareness   **2. Self-Dislosure**   **3. Listening**
(Thoughts and Feelings)   **(Verbal and Nonverbal)**

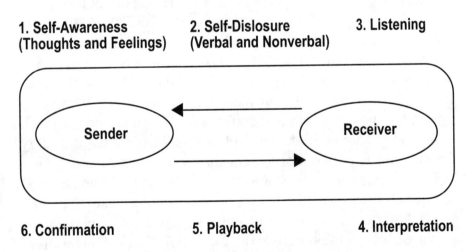

Sender   **Receiver**

6. Confirmation   **5. Playback**   **4. Interpretation**

Figure 5: The Process of Communication

The process of communication involves a "sender" and a "receiver"—someone who encodes and someone who decodes the message sent. Both of these individuals need to exercise specific skills, for connection and understanding to occur without interference. They both need an attitude of respect and the skills of attending and concreteness for effective communication to take place. The sender (encoder) needs to be able to self-disclose with openness and honesty, and the receiver (decoder) needs the skills of emphatic listening and the ability to create a safe and receptive context in which understanding can occur.

The six stages outlined in Figure 5 (previous page) illustrate the various steps that need to occur in the transfer of information from one person to another in order for them to achieve connection and experience a shared sense of meaning. These six stages actually highlight the six skills crucial in the process of making connection: self-awareness, self-disclosure, listening, interpretation, playback, and confirmation. What follows is a brief description of each skill and the part it plays in the communication process.

Self-Awareness: There are two essential beginning points for all couple communication. The first relates to our ability to be aware of and in touch with or own thoughts and feelings. The second involves an awareness of how we feel about others. If we see ourselves as inadequate, inferior, or insecure, this will surely affect the way we encode our messages to others. If we see others as uncaring, unsupportive, and aggressive, this will also shape the process of encoding. Being able successfully to encode the messages we wish to send to our marriage partner is vitally affected by our feelings of worth and self-esteem. If we are not in touch with who we are and how we feel, we may have great difficulty formulating what we really want to say to others. Feelings not acknowledged cannot be shared. Some other factors can also distort our ability to reveal what we want to communicate to others: our lack of expressiveness; our ambivalence about certain issues; or our active intention to hide or cover up feelings of anger, frustration, fear, dominance, or deception.[8]

Self-Disclosure: Self-disclosure is a significant component in the process of communication. It involves verbally sharing our private thoughts, ideas, attitudes, and beliefs and provides the basis for an emotional expressiveness that increases rapport and strengthens the potential of the relationship with another person. It also involves nonverbal sharing, which can include a shared, meaningful glance; an affectionate touch; shared emotional expressions such as tears or laughter; and shared sexuality.[9]

The importance of the nonverbal dimension of self-disclosure is grossly underestimated by many couples who are simply unaware of the powerful impact that messages received through this mode of expression have on their experience of intimacy. It is generally agreed that nonverbal communication accounts for about 93 percent of the message communicated, with only 7 percent of the message being contained in the actual words. Fifty-five percent of the message is transmitted through the body language or "visual aspects" (facial expression, gaze, posture, gestures) and 38 percent by means of the "vocal aspects" (tone of voice, loudness, tempo, pitch). Furthermore, the nonverbal aspects of the communication are extremely important to marital couples, because they are the vehicle through which expressions of emotion, interpersonal attitudes of respect and empathy, and feelings about the relationship are all conveyed.[10]

Listening: Undoubtedly, listening is the most important communication skill, because it is the means by which we are affirmed as understood and acceptable. Nothing deflates and hurts us more than being ignored or cut off. Michael Nichols believes that listening is a very powerful force in all of our lives, because it enables us to immerse ourselves in the experience of another person. He sees listening as a gift by which we give our attention and understanding to others, making them feel validated and valued. Effective listening, he asserts, creates good will and provides the best way for us to enjoy and learn from others. Through listening, couples can build bonds of understanding that strengthen their relationship and connect them to each other.[11]

Interpretation: Empathic listening has the ability to draw us into the private world of others and provide them with a sense of safety and receptivity. Connected to the skill of listening is the need to interpret accurately the message being sent. What are you saying? What does it mean? The skill of decoding, to be successful, needs to be used in a way that shows a sensitivity and responsiveness to what matters most to the sender—decoding effectively their feelings and grasping the meaning and significance of their communication. Nothing is more validating to a marriage partner than the feeling that they have been heard and understood accurately.

Breakdowns occur at any one of the six stages in the communication process, but no stage is more critical than the interpretation stage. Knowing that your partner understands how you think and feel is the heart of making connection. However, disconnection is common, and there are many reasons why effective communication breaks down due to faulty decoding of the message. Factors responsible for these interferences or breakdowns can include: words or meanings that are ambiguous; our attitude toward our partner; assumptions we make about the topic/issue that shows our preconceived biases or prejudices; emotional defensiveness that is triggered by our self-absorption or feelings of hurt, fear, or anger; interrupting or jumping to conclusions; and the past history of the relationship.[12]

Playback: The third part of the listening process involves what is often referred to as "reflective listening." This playing back to the sender our understanding of what they have just said is a very useful tool in the process of communicating our understanding. Here we check to see that we got the message accurately and reassure the sender that we have taken seriously the things they have been saying. As Hugh MacKay says, "Reflective listening is the restraint which ensures that we will receive a message before we react to it; if our playback is inaccurate—either in content or tone—this gives the speaker an opportunity to correct our understanding of what has been said."[13] The most effective method to use in playing back what we have heard is to paraphrase the total message—content and feelings—so the sender can confirm that what they said has been "read" accurately.

Confirmation: The process of communication is completed when the sender confirms that connection has been made and the listener has accurately heard the message and acknowledged the reality of their feelings. This act of confirmation is a moment of agreement that creates a feeling of emotional intensity and conveys the sender's appreciation, acceptance, and affirmation for the support and understanding that has been achieved. It greatly increases the sense of emotional bonding and the level of intimacy experienced in the relationship. If confirmation is not offered, this provides the opportunity for the sender and receiver to try again to see if connection can be achieved.

Understanding the six stages of the communication process highlights two very important issues for marital communication that need to be underscored. The first is the important part that nonverbal communication plays in the process of emotional bonding. Receiving the total message that is sent not only ensures a greater understanding but provides the key to emotional connection. A failure to decode the nuances of feeling transmitted through the nonverbal channel greatly inhibits the prospects for intimacy and dwarfs the potential for emotional closeness in the marriage. So often in marriage, communication takes place at the content level, but getting to the deeper levels of feelings and meaning does not occur, because couples fail to listen carefully to *all* that is being communicated.

The second issue relates to the crucial role that listening skills play in the process of marital communication. Poor listening is one of the most significant problems facing marital partners in their relationship with each other. Evidence suggests that listening actually constitutes at least 50 percent of all communication, yet we use only 25 percent of our listening capacity. That means that we actually screen out, ignore, distort, or misunderstand about 75 percent of all that we hear every day.

The Art of Listening

As we have already noted, listening is one of the greatest gifts we can give to another person. It is an act of love and caring, and with it we convey a very powerful message of affirmation about the value we attach to the individual speaking to us.

Listening is important to us for a number of reasons. First, it is the way we receive information about others, our relationships, our world, and even ourselves. Second, it is the means whereby we validate the experiences of others and they recognize and validate our experiences. Third, it nourishes our self-worth and helps us feel lovable, acceptable, and worthwhile as human beings. Fourth, it has the ability to shape our character and make us feel secure. Finally, it is the bridge between the spaces that divide or separate us from others. We all yearn to escape the isolation of our existence—to find community in the land of understanding.

Dietrich Bonhoeffer, in his book, *Life Together,* talks of listening as a ministry. He says that the first service we owe to others consists of listening to them—that loving another person means learning to listen to them. Yet so often as Christians, we feel we must always contribute something to others, thus forgetting that "listening can be a greater service than speaking."[15] He then goes on to say:

> Many people are looking for an ear that will listen. They do not find it among Christians, because these Christians are talking where they should be listening. But he who can not longer listen to his brother will soon be no longer listening to God either; we will be doing nothing but prattle in the presence of God too. This is the beginning of the death of the Spiritual life.[16]

The Bible writers also confirm the importance of listening. Solomon said that "the wise listen to others" (Proverbs 12:15, NLT) and that "answering before listening is both stupid and rude" (Proverbs 18:13, *THE MESSAGE*). The apostle James admonished everyone in the early Christian church to "be quick to listen and slow to speak" (James 1:19, NIV).

So why is it that we all find it so hard to listen? Nichols suggests that "to listen well, we must forget ourselves and submit to the other person's need for attention"[17]—and that is not easy. Being preoccupied with our own immediate needs and concerns does prevent us from listening. There are, of course, many different reasons why we find it so difficult to listen. Some of the common reasons for our failure to listen are:

1. **Inattention** due to fatigue or busyness—listening requires focused attention, energy, and effort.

2. **Preoccupation** with our own thoughts, feelings, work, or needs.

3. **Distraction**—either by our own inner dialogue, by noise or activity levels, or by trigger words or emotions generated by the dialogue.

4. **Information overload**—too much information, or information we don't understand (e.g.: technical language).

5. **Actively and intentionally blocking** the communication process by filtering out what we don't want to hear, changing the subject, blaming the other person, busily rehearsing what to say in response, or giving a solution prematurely.

6. **Boredom**—"I've heard all this before!"

7. **Making assumptions** or snap judgments about what or how something is being said.

8. Being focused on the details of the story and **missing the feelings and emotions being expressed.**

According to Carl Rogers, being a good listener requires being actively involved in the process of dialogue. He made a clear distinction between "passive listening" and what he called "active listening." Passively listening, he said, involves merely hearing the topic or monologue of a speaker, whereas "active listening" involves two people engaged in interacting together, each listening intently and trying to understand and respond to what the other person is saying. Rogers believed that this process of active listening involved three key components:

Listening to words and feelings. The listener pays close attention to hearing not only what is being said (the words) but hearing and understanding the feelings behind the words as well.

Empathizing with the speaker. Empathy is all about understanding and responding to the emotional experience of the other person. It involves listeners in perceiving with sensitivity what the other person is seeing and feeling by putting themselves in the position of the speaker and seeing the world through their eyes. It also means that the listener develops the capacity to let the other person know that they are understood and respected.

Suspending judgment. The listener accepts the thoughts and feelings expressed by the speaker without making any judgments or condemnations. This means that the listener will need to suspend his or her own value judgments and receive the whole message before reacting to it. It suggests that the listener is willing to allow the other person's feelings to exist with any attempt to avoid, deny, fix, control, or invalidate them.

Learning the art of actively listening is a skill that should be taught to all couples, whether married or planning to get married. All couples need to learn how to "tune into" their partner and sharpen their ability to hear accurately. It is often hard for us to be objective about how well we listen, because we are frequently blind to the bad habits we have developed that prevent us from maintaining our focus and attending to the message being delivered. In addition, we find it hard to believe that our own anxiety to please or control could be the reason why our responses block the communication process. If we do get to hear all that is being said, we frequently go and spoil it all by saying something or jumping in and giving our response before we have had a chance to check whether we clearly understood what our partner was trying to say to us.

Here then, are a few signs of a good listener:

1. Maintains good eye contact with the person speaking.

2. Responds with a smile or nod of the head, or shows concern.

3. Pays close attention "to all that is going on."

4. Does not interrupt the flow of information.

5. Maintains an open, accepting attitude and posture.

6. Learns to listen (even in the silences) and does not push the pace or rush the speaker.

7. Is empathetic—able to put oneself in the other person's shoes.

8. Remains poised and emotionally controlled.

9. Does not change the topic, but allows the speaker to finish expressing his or her thoughts.

10. Connects with the other's feelings; repeats those parts of the message not clearly understood; clarifies and reflects back the thoughts and feelings of the speaker by using a paraphrase of what has been said.

On Being Assertive

If good relationships depend on how well we listen and connect with each other, then it is equally true to say that the quality and vitality of the marriage is dependent on how well the couple is able to express their feelings to each other. Intimate relationships depend on both active listening and assertiveness. Active listening is about empathizing, accepting, and understanding the self-revelations offered to us by our partner. Assertiveness is about being willing to disclose openly to our partner what we feel, need, or desire. If either of these skills are underdeveloped or missing from our relationship, then the marriage will be superficial, unfulfilling, and miserable.[18]

Because many people have difficulty sharing their feelings, they find it hard to be assertive, and their relationships tend to suffer and fall short of their potential as a result. Sharing feelings takes courage and usually occurs only when we feel safe and secure within ourselves and in our relationship with our partner. A number of influential factors tend to inhibit or prevent the effective expression and sharing of feelings and diminish the prospects for achieving intimacy. First, our basic instinctual response to any problem or difficulty is either *fight* (aggression) or *flight* (passivity). No one teaches us how to master the skill of being assertive. Second, we are afraid of being ridiculed or rejected if we reveal how we feel. We do not want to risk being seen as inadequate or inferior. Third, we lack confidence in ourselves and doubt that we are really worthwhile or lovable. We find it much easier to pretend that we feel OK about ourselves and hope that other people will love us for what we pretend to be. Finally, we have grown up with no positive role models to teach us how to identify, access, or express our feelings.[19]

World-renowned family therapist Virginia Satir taught that the pathway to better communication begins with learning how to make contact with others by sharing feelings and concerns in an open, honest way. She maintains that people who have a low opinion of themselves and feel that they are unlovable tend to mask or hide these feelings and communicate with others in ways that are either passive (nonassertive), aggressive, or indirect (passive-aggressive). According to her experience, she believes that less than 5 percent of people are really comfortable with who they are and willing to be emotionally honest and communicate assertively. This suggests that in most conversations, there is not much of a personal or private nature being disclosed or shared between people, so the chances of intimacy are greatly reduced.

Satir described four ways of communicating that individuals typically use to exert influence over others and manage their inner feelings in their attempt to survive both physically and emotionally. She labeled these four styles as:

Placating—giving up ourselves so that people will love us enough to let us live.

Blaming—forcing others to obey us so that we feel safe, at least for the moment.

Super-reasonable—drowning people with words, boring them with endless explanations, and frustrating them by showing no feelings.

Being irrelevant—keeping people so busy by introducing so many unconnected things that they feel dizzy, distracted, and help-less.[20]

Being assertive is about defining who we are ("the self") and defending our personal and private space. It involves allowing me to take ownership of my own thoughts, feelings, and desires and feeling free to express them. It means allowing me to take responsibility for determining my own personal boundaries and defining how close I want other people to be to me. Being assertive means that I have a right to honor and respect who I am and to prevent others from belittling, denigrating, manipulating, and controlling my life. But it also means that I have a responsibility to honor, respect, and affirm the rights of others to be who they are too, and not to violate their personhood.

Implications for Marriage

There are obvious implications here for how we behave and communicate in marriage. Frequently, lack of assertiveness in marriage allows couples to dishonor and disrespect each other in ways that block or destroy the process of intimacy. Marriage partners often use tactics designed to get them what they want or to get their own way.

Such tactics are designed to prevent the partner from having a choice or a chance to state opinions, feelings, or desires. The partner will often feel trapped by such domination and manipulation and will give up, fearing only rejection or ridicule if they try to express their opinions or oppose the proposed course of action.

Assertiveness is a way for couples to make their relationship more equal, enjoyable, and emotionally honest. They need to be encouraged to invest in improving the quality of their relationship and developing a greater sense of emotional closeness by learning how to be more assertive and communicating in ways that facilitate emotional connection. Many Christian couples may feel at this point that some of their basic assumptions and life principles around the issues of the denial of self, the ownership and expression of feelings (especially the need to suppress negative feelings) and the equality of roles are challenged by the notions of assertiveness.

However, we need to remember that the Christian way of life clearly requires that we not only have confidence in God's love but that we recognize that He asks us to act responsibly and communicate with each other in ways that are open, honest, and genuine. We acknowledge that most of the problems we encounter and most of the unhappiness that we experience is due largely to a

	Nonassertive	Assertive	Aggressive
Characteristic Behavior	• Indirect • Self-denying • Emotionally dishonest • Self-sabotaging	• Direct • Self-enhancing • Emotionally honest	• Direct • Self-defeating • Emotionally honest (inappropriately) • Self-enhancing at others' expense
How you feel when you engage in this behavior	• Hurt • Anxious now; angry later	• Confident • Self-respecting	• Superior • Self-righteous
How others feel toward you when you engage in this behavior	• Irritation • Pity • Disgust	• Respect • Appreciation	• Anger • Vengefulness
Nonverbal signs	• Whiny voice • Downcast eyes • Stooped posture	• Calm voice • Direct eye contact • Relaxed posture	• Loud, shouting voice • Pointing finger • Stiff posture
Key words	• Maybe • Sorry • But	• I think • I feel • I want	• You'd better • Should, ought • Come on

Table 3: A comparison of Nonassertive, Assertive, and Aggressive Behaviors, adapted from *Assert Yourself,* by Gail Lindenfield (1986) and "An Introduction to Assertiveness Training," by American Personal and Guidance Association (1973)

lack of communication that occurs when people fail to express what they want, think, or feel.

To start with, couples may wish to enhance their personhood and self-worth by exploring and embracing the concept of "freedom to be," which is expressed in the five freedoms enumerated by Virginia Satir:

1. The freedom to *see and hear what is here* instead of what should be, was, or will be.

2. The freedom to *say what one feels and thinks,* instead of what one should.

3. The freedom to *feel what one feels,* instead of what one ought.

4. The freedom to *ask for what one wants,* instead of always waiting for permission.

5. The freedom to *take risks* on one's own behalf, instead of choosing to be only "secure" and not rocking the boat.[21]

Couples may also like to recognize the various dimensions involved in understanding and developing assertive behaviors by examining the differences outlined in Table 3 (facing page).

In order for couples to develop more specifically the skills of communicating assertively, they may wish to explore some of the following methods:

▶ Self-awareness of personal thoughts and feelings.

▶ Learning how to express positive and negative feelings.

▶ How to give and receive positive recognition/affirmation.

▶ Learning how to formulate and utilize "I" messages (which play a large part in assertive behavior).

▶ Giving and receiving good quality feedback.

▶ Ways to successfully negotiate.

▶ How to develop self-protective skills to deal with criticism, put-downs, and manipulation.

Gender Differences in Marital Communication

We come now to another very significant aspect of communication that influences a couple's quest for intimacy in marriage. Because, as we have been emphasizing, the communication process is primarily about the exchange of feelings, it is important for us to recognize that men and women come to understand each other and evaluate the quality of their relationship by the quantity of feelings they freely express to each other. For this reason, the differences between the way men and women seem to approach relationships, and in particular, marital communication, demands our attention.

The fact is that "scholars have arguably paid more attention to gender-related factors and gender differences than to any other contextual factors in marital communication."[22] While not wanting to stereotype men and women's behaviors, what has emerged from the research is a recognition of the fact that men and women do have different interactional goals in relationships, and these give rise to separate and distinct gender-related patterns that are observable in most male-female relationships. Of course, nobody knows for sure whether these differences and patterns are the result of our genetic history or our social conditioning, but regardless of their origins, a failure to understand and accommodate them frequently lies at the bottom of a lot of marital problems and difficulties. Howard Markman, Director of the University of Denver's Center for Marital and Family Studies, once commented that "misunderstood gender differences are one of the greatest causes of divorce."[23]

Deborah Tannen, a leading linguistics expert, believes that we need to understand how men and women use very different conversational styles and that the talk between them is best understood as cross-cultural communication.[24] This clash of conversational styles she refers to not as dialects but as "genderlects," in which "women speak and hear a language of connection and intimacy, while men speak and hear a language of status and independence."[25] Researchers agree that women tend to perceive themselves primarily in relation to the people around them and that their sense of self comes from this relatedness. They tend to be habitually focused outward and have fascination with and concern for others and their needs. Men, on the other hand, tend to be self-focused and concerned with achieving status, independence, and avoiding failure.

These different approaches to communicating by men and women bring to light a range of significant differences that affect the way a couple interprets each other's messages and how they go about providing help, solving problems, and giving protection to each other. Women, for example, are often accused of talking too much, interrupting and overlapping others in conversation, and nagging or repeatedly making the same request. Men, of course, are purported to being strong and silent and frequently interpret repeated requests to do something as a threat to their ability to choose and be in control of things.

On the other hand, men tend to listen to woman's problems and impatiently offer them solutions, whereas, when a woman talks about a problem, she is requesting understanding and connectedness. For women, talk is the glue that holds relationships together; for men, relationships are held together by action. Conflict is a necessary means by which status is negotiated for men, but for most women, conflict presents a threat to connection and should be avoided at all costs. Most women feel that connection is more important than respect, whereas for men, respect from others is more important than intimacy.

Cris Evatt, in her book *He and She*, outlines sixty differences between men and women that are cited by the researchers. Listed in Table 4 (following page) is a rather concise summary of many of these differences, particularly those that relate to marital communication and intimacy. While some sociologists tend to see these basic differences in terms of a power struggle between the sexes, the real issue seems to relate more to the way that men and women resolve the relational polarities of intimacy and independence, connection and status, and connectedness and separateness. The dilemma for all of us is that the experience of intimacy and connectedness requires that we are simultaneously aware of our need for separateness and independence, which is achieved through the process of individuation.

Men, it seems, need more distance or separateness in a relationship, yet find it hard to tell their partner when they feel smothered or engulfed. Women, on the other hand, tend to define themselves by and through relationships and feel a sense of abandonment and isolation when a man cannot handle closeness.

Women tend to:	Men tend to:
Be other focused	Be self-focused
Be more cooperative	Be more competitive
Over-identify with people	Over-identify with work
Need more closeness	Need more distance
Fear abandonment	Fear engulfment
Talk mostly about people	Talk mostly about things
Be more indirect in speaking	Be more direct in speaking
Search more for hidden meanings	Take words at face value
Like to talk a problem out and take time with decisions	Be more decisive and solve problems immediately
Be better listeners	Struggle for dominance and control of conversation
Avoid intimidation	Attempt to intimidate
Avoid conflict and confrontations	Like conflict, power struggles, and confronting others
Admit wrongs and self-blame	Apologize only when it's expected and unavoidable
Be more comfortable expressing their emotions	Be taught not to show emotion
Repress their anger	Express their anger
Be less afraid of commitment	Fear or avoid commitment
Want more love in relationships	Want more sex in relationships
Be more giving	Be more cautious and conscious of what they'll get
Seek the approval of others	Do more what pleases them
Be emotionally jealous and fear loss of emotional commitment	Be more sexually jealous and fear loss of control

Table 4: Basic Differences Between Men and Women

Carol Gilligan, Professor of Gender Studies at Harvard University, suggests that "male gender identity is threatened by intimacy, while female identity is threatened by separation. Thus males tend to have difficulty with intimate relationships, while females tend to have problems with individuation."[27]

All this discussion highlights the need for marital couples to be consciously aware, not only of these differences, but of the need for them to understand and connect with each other through the process of communication. A failure to understand and connect at the emotional level is the major reason a lot of marriages struggle to survive.

When misunderstanding does occur, most couples stop listening to each other and become defensive and unreceptive to new information. Typically, a negative cycle emerges in which low levels of information, disclosure, or assertiveness result in misunderstandings, which in turn produce anxiety, resistance, and sometimes over-reaction to attempts to hear or clarify new ideas and perceptions or empathize with the feelings of the other person.

This cycle of negativity elicits from us some of our most deep-seated fears and anxieties. Most of us come to marriage with a range of learned behavior which we use to protect ourselves from hurt—and which covers up our fears when sharing ourselves with others becomes too risky or painful. Individuals learn to bottle up their feelings in an effort to hide their fears of being criticized or ridiculed.

Hatfield suggests that the fears that cause most anxiety and lead to misunderstanding and emotional blockages in the communication process are:

1. **Fear of exposure**—not wanting others to get too close to find out what is wrong or shameful about us.

2. **Fear of abandonment**—concern that when the shameful things about us are exposed, we will be abandoned.

3. **Fear that our vulnerabilities will be used** by our partner against us either to denounce, criticize, or belittle us.

4. **Fear of loss of control**—being unable to control strong emotional reactions by others or ourselves.

5. **Fear of one's own destructive impulse**—the need to keep our intense emotional feelings hidden or bottled up, for fear of destroying ourselves or our relationship with others.

6. **Fear of being engulfed**—when persons feel they cannot genuinely reveal their thoughts, feelings, or values without being overwhelmed by another's response. It also occurs when one cannot listen to another person's feelings or wants, for fear of being obligated to sacrifice oneself completely to fulfil them.[28]

For couples to be able to communicate effectively with each other, they need to be willing to reveal their inner feelings and risk extending themselves beyond those areas where they feel comfortable and unafraid. They also need to be prepared to make it safe for their partner to communicate with and respond to them with empathy, acceptance, and trust. One very good way they can begin to extend themselves is to make a point of telling each other about positive feelings, as these are easily accepted and present little risk.

This action will tend to increase the opportunity for intimacy by reducing fears and inhibitions—and create a climate in which it will be easier to reveal other feelings that are more difficult to share.

Notes:

1. Karen J. Prager, *The Psychology of Intimacy* (New York: Guilford Press, 1995), p. 57.

2. Mark A. Whisman, "Satisfaction in Close Relationships," in *Satisfaction in Close Relationships*, by Robert Sternberg and Mahzad Hojjat (New York: Guilford Press, 1997), p. 395.

3   Judith Feeney, Patricia Noller, and Carla Ward, "Marital Satisfaction and Spousal Interaction," in *Satisfaction in Close Relationships*, by Robert Sternberg and Mahzad Hojjat, (New York: Guilford Press, 1997), p. 160.

4.   Ibid., pp. 161, 162.

5   Patricia Noller, *Nonverbal Communication and Marital Interaction* (Oxford: Pergamon Press, 1984), p. 1.

6.   Stephen R. Covey, *The 7 Habits of Highly Effective People* (New York: Simon and Schuster, Inc., 1989), pp. 236-260.

7.   Powell, John, *Why Am I Afraid to Tell You Who I Am?* (Illinois: Argus Communications, 1960), pp. 50-62.

8.   Patricia Noller, *Nonverbal Communication and Marital Interaction*, p. 71.

9.   Karen J. Prager, *The Psychology of Intimacy,* p. 21.

10.   Patricia Noller, *Nonverbal Communication and Marital Interaction*, pp. 5-7.

11.   Michael P. Nichols, *The Lost Art of Listening* (New York: Guilford Press,1995), pp. 4, 6, 10.

12.   Patricia Noller, *Nonverbal Communication and Marital Interaction,* pp. 72, 185.

13.   Hugh Mackay, *Why Don't People Listen?* (Sydney: Pan MacMillan Publishers, 1994), p. 178.

14.   Michael P. Nichols, *The Lost Art of Listening*, pp. 15, 16.

15.   Dietrich Bonhoeffer, *Life Together* (London: SCM Press, Ltd., 1954), p. 75.

16.   Ibid., p. 75.

17.   Michael P. Nichols, *The Lost Art of Listening*, p. 3.

18.   See Robert Bolton, *People Skills* (New Jersey: Prentice Hall, Inc., 1979), p. 118.

19.   Christy Lane and Laura Ann Stevens, *How to Stay Married* (London: Arrow Books, 1991), pp. 88-97.

20.   Virginia Satir, *Making Contact* (California: Celestial Arts, 1976), p. 14.

21. Ibid.

22. Karen J. Prager, *The Psychology of Intimacy,* pp., 214, 215.

23. Cris Evatt, *He and She* (California: Canari Press, 1992), p. 7.

24. Deborah Tannen, *You Just Don't Understand* (Australia: Random House, 1990), p 18.

25. Ibid., p. 42.

26. Cris Evatt, *He and She*, pp. 150, 151.

27. Carol Gilligan, *In a Different Voice* (Cambridge: University Press, 1982), p. 62.

28. Jon Carlson and Len Sperry, *The Intimate Couple* (Philadelphia: Brunner/Mazel, 1999), pp. 116, 117.

FOUR

Sexual Intimacy

S exual intimacy constitutes a foundational part of the marriage relationship. It plays a central role in our understanding of how love and intimacy grow and develop between two people. It reflects the commitment and emotional bonding that marital partners experience with one another and symbolizes the sense of unity, interdependence, pleasure, communion, and creativity they aspire to achieve.

The Role of Sex in Intimacy

When a couple join together in sexual love, they engage in what is undoubtedly the most powerful means possible of experiencing love and tenderness and creating a sense of unity and mutuality. The sexual experience has the ability to bridge the differences of thought and experience between two people and move them from isolation and loneliness to the place where they can comfortably commune with each other and enjoy feelings of mutual trust and acceptance. This experience also becomes an ongoing source of intense pleasure and a way for marital partners to communicate intimately about each other's needs, drives, and emotions. Through the intense rhythms of lovemaking, a couple create a deep bond with each other and come to surrender the mystery of their personhood and reveal their most cherished and hidden secrets.[1]

However, the great tragedy is that so much of our current approach to human sexuality continually and deliberately divorces it from the emotional development of the individual or the couple and concentrates only on performance and sexual technique—on descriptions of sexuality as biological process, orgasmic catharsis, and narcissistic fulfilment. When we embrace sex only as performance, passion, and positions, it becomes superficial, exploitative, and degrading—cut off from our deepest yearnings for intimacy and connection. Human sexual behavior must be seen as part of a bigger process. It must be seen as a multi-layered emotional experience that is the very essence of our being—a desire to form an intimate union with another where love and caring transcend self-interest and create emotional connection and fulfilment. This emotional connection transforms an impersonal biological process into an act of love and provides the grounds for intimacy in the marriage.[2]

Since the sexual revolution of the 1960s, western culture has been engrossed in the process of challenging and redefining traditional beliefs, values, and practices about human sexual behavior. While social scientists and sex researchers like William Masters and Virginia Johnson[3] have done a lot to dispel many of the myths and misconceptions that surround our understanding of human sexual behaviors, many still exist. It is true that, in spite of the fact that many people feel "liberated" from the repressed sexual beliefs and practices of the past, our present society has over-reacted and swung in the other direction, using new perspectives to glorify sex and enslave us with a mythology that is as equally binding and repressive as it was in the past. Today, sex has been demystified and fully secularized, to the extent that it is seen as a matter of self-gratification, pleasure, and self-exploration—a wonderful recreational sport that is clearly mistaken for emotional intimacy and connectedness.

How we decide issues of sexual morality and develop a more integrated, healthy, and wholesome view of our own sexuality will no doubt continue to be a central feature of our cultural landscape. However, in this chapter we want to see how attitudes toward sex, that have been influential within the Christian church over the centuries, have impacted Christian couples and created many obstacles that have prevented them from coming to a healthy view of sexuality. We also want to explore a biblical understanding of sex as a gift from God and how sexuality is closely connected to our spirituality. Then, finally, we discuss some of the emotional aspects of human sexual responses and outline how couples can achieve sexual satisfaction in their marriage.

Human Sexuality and the Christian Church

Throughout history, the Christian church has expressed great concern about issues of human sexuality, particularly highlighting the evils of the immoral sexual life. Consistently, it has promoted negative views about sexuality, leading many to view sex with distaste and suspicion. The church has, at times, even deplored that God ever created sex and ordained it as a means of procreation, because it considered sex to be shameful and a hindrance to the holy life.

These attitudes toward human sexuality date back to the postapostolic age, when, during the infancy of the early Christian church, a radical change occurred in its teachings regarding sex and marriage. Influenced more or less by a number of cultic, theological, and cultural movements of the day, the church began to allow negative attitudes to emerge as it moved away from the "naturalism" of the Old Testament and the culture of Judaism that had developed around it. Scholars reflecting on these changes attribute them to four major factors:

1. The dualism in Hellenistic thought which asserted that human beings were made up of two parts: body and spirit. The body was believed to provide a temporary "vehicle," as it were, for the external spirit to ride around in. The spirit was the superior part of the person and something to be prized; the body was the lower or animal component, something definitely to be despised. (Consequently, sex was tolerated only for procreation.)

2. The asceticism that was common to many pagan religions and philosophies of the day claimed that a holy, pure, or perfect life could only be achieved by self-denial and withdrawal from the world. Being free of physical desire symbolized the achievement of self-humiliation.

3. The pagan licentiousness of the Greco-Roman world caused the church to enforce clear standards of sexual behavior.

4. The mistaken belief that the apostle Paul supported the idea of a body/spirit dualism (Romans 8:35, 36) and that his statement "it is well for man not to touch a woman" (1 Corinthians 7:1), suggested that he believed that the body, and therefore sex, is evil and dangerous. (In fact, Paul nowhere declares that marriage is evil or that sex is unclean. His case for sexual abstinence was based not on dualism but on an argument that is apocalyptic in nature).[4]

The distorted and negative views about sex and marriage that developed within Christianity during these early years have shaped Christian thought for centuries. By the post-Nicene period, Augustine had further confused church teachings with his unbiblical speculations, claiming that original sin was to be equated with sexual desire, which was punishment for the fall. Every act of sexual intercourse was therefore shameful, tainted with evil, and fundamentally disgusting. He also taught that marriage was a necessary but distasteful means of propagating the human race and constituted a concession to the weakness instilled in human beings through their primal disobedience; that the suppression of one's sex life was a positive good because it actually caused both anguish and guilt; and that virginity, celibacy, and self-denial were meritorious works and therefore pathways to knowing God.[5]

During the Middle Ages, these ideas became further entrenched with the rise of monasticism and the influence of Thomas Aquinas. Through his writings, Aquinas bought together the two streams of dualism and naturalism into one well-reasoned philosophy of sex and marriage. His work, which was totally foreign to the teachings of scripture, provided a maze of rational arguments and fine distinctions that codified all actions regarding sexual behavior. Such moral judgments served only to increase the potential for greater frustration, legalism, neurotic guilt, shame, and humiliation in sexual matters.[6]

The Reformation period which followed saw a reaction against the views held by Thomas Aquinas, with Luther challenging the belief that redemption takes place only when the soul/spirit is released from the sinful body by abstinence and self-denial. Luther taught that sex was a gift of God, that the body as such is not sinful, and that the beautiful instinct of sex has been spoiled by the devil. He opposed celibacy and saw the use of sex within marriage as natural, necessary, and normative. Furthermore, he focused on the total personality (body, soul, and spirit) and taught that the sexual side of life is not to be denied or repressed but used properly as God intended, within the confines of marriage.

During the nineteenth century, sexual attitudes and practices came to be influenced by a curious blending of puritanism, pietism, and rationalism. The Puritans emphasized moderation in all things and stressed loyalty to God as their supreme motive. Monogamy and a single standard of sexual morality agreed with their goals of honest labor, devotion to duty, and economic success.

The Pietists sought very much to live a holy life and believed that only those who avoided the practices and pleasures of the world gave evidence of their regeneration. It is generally accepted that the influence of the Pietists served to soften the prevailing crudity and vulgarity and reduce the intemperance and immorality of their times. However, they tended to associate sex with sin and a bad conscience, in spite of the fact that they acknowledged that marriage was approved of God.

The Rationalists—who substituted reason for the authority of scripture and refused to accept any moral standards except those established by nature, reason, and experience—advocated a return to natural religion and humanistic morality. They became the forerunners of the sexual libertinism that inspired the sexual revolution of the 1960s and 1970s. These times led to a reexamination of sexual ethics and to a more open and affirming approach toward sexuality. Yet, in spite of this openness and acceptance, our post-modernist culture also falls into the trap of dualistic thinking about sexuality. It proclaims that sexual pleasure is good and should be experienced by all with uninhibited enjoyment, yet it severs sexuality from marriage and makes sex a legitimate goal in its own right. This attitude of "untrammeled naturalism" makes sex an absolute and once again erects a barrier to healthy sexual attitudes by dividing the human person into parts which are understood to be in conflict with one another.

When you make an idol of sex, you denigrate love into lust and sex into sensuality.[7] It is not difficult to see how the Christian church has provided us with a mixed legacy of ideas regarding human sexuality. Having inherited a fractured view of human nature, the post-modern church continues to articulate a confused and inadequate corpus of teaching regarding the body, sexuality, marriage, and issues of gender difference and equality. In spite of the fact that Jesus and Paul shattered many of the excesses of Hellenistic thought and reaffirmed a basically Judaistic approach to sexuality, the church is still struggling to embrace healthy views of sexuality.

The real tragedy of church history is that a whole range of nonbiblical ideas and influences have been allowed to eclipse and dominate the truth about our personhood and our sexual natures. The cultural biases and the faulty interpretations of scripture by the church fathers over the years have obscured the simple truths expressed in the Bible. The failure of the church over the years to develop an accurate understanding and appreciation for the sexual side of human beings has not only prevented men and women from enjoying their differences but has been used to inhibit, restrict, and even abuse relational growth and happiness.

A Biblical Understanding of the Gift of Human Sexuality

To be human is be sexual. This means that we are born as either male or female, masculine or feminine. Furthermore, we understand that our sexuality, which is a gift from the Creator-God, comes with a built-in capacity to give and receive pleasure, emotional support, and spiritual fulfilment.

Most of this understanding about human sexuality has its genesis in the biblical story of creation, in which God is seen making human beings in His own image as male and female. This creative act on the part of God provides the basis for us to define who we are (personhood) and how we should relate to each other. It implies that God designed us to be social and relational beings capable of communion with our Creator and possessing a specific capacity for experiencing intimacy in relationship with each other.

When God created male and female at the completion of His creative work, He declared that both beings were "very good" (Genesis 1:31, NIV). This ultimate expression of His creative genius evoked His deepest satisfaction and most passionate acclamation. God was truly excited! There was no ambivalence here about what He had just done. There was nothing unclean, shameful, or incomplete about His work at all—it was "very good."

The only thing that was "not good" in this creation story was Adam's loneliness and separation. He had been given lordship over creation, but he lacked companionship—he needed a "helpmeet" (Genesis 2:18). This lack stood to violate the principle of relatedness so essential to God's plan for community. So, God created the female to complement the male. They both came into existence with a built-in longing and desire for each other, not just physically and sexually, but socially, emotionally, psychologically, and spiritually as well.

The bible record suggests that Adam sensed immediately how Eve complemented him. In the moment they met for the first time, the sense of yearning for true partnership and communion that lingered in Adam's heart and soul burst forth into joyous exclamation: "YES!" "At Last!" (See Genesis 2:23.) He now had a companion, a counterpart, someone capable of meeting his needs, someone corresponding to his being, someone equal to him but different (because love cannot be a mere self-reflection. (See Genesis 2:18, 23.)

Here there is no suggestion of any hierarchy of genders. Male and female accept each other equally as image bearers of God, responsible to God for the well-being of the creation and each a biological and social complement of the other. Stuart Barton Babbage, in his book *Sex and Sanity,* says, "The Bible lends no support to the mythical view that human beings were originally androgynous. Man, according to the Bible exists in a state of sexual polarity, of complimentary differentiation, by the will of God, by the fact that 'male and female created He them.'"[8]

Here the Genesis record clearly identifies sexuality as God's idea. It certainly was no accident or afterthought. Human sexuality, like everything else that God had created, reflected a design that was purposeful, wise, and good. Obviously, it was a valuable and intentional gift from God, given to men and women, to be embraced and celebrated with gratitude, joy, and delight.

If Genesis affirms our sexuality, then the Song of Solomon celebrates it. Here in this Old Testament book, we experience the songs of love that flourish as two lovers celebrate the orchestrated symphony of human love and delight in the rapturous joy of marital intimacy and emotional connectedness. Here we see sensuality without licentiousness, passion without promiscuity, and love without lust. It is a story that portrays love's intensity, restraint, mutuality, and permanence within the covenant relationship of marriage.[9]

In New Testament times, Jesus reaffirmed a very positive view of sex and marriage when He upheld the "one flesh" teaching of the creation narrative (Matthew 19:6). Furthermore, when He was challenged with a question by the Scribes and Pharisees about marital unfaithfulness, He declared that even looking at a woman lustfully amounted to committing adultery already in one's own heart (Matthew 5:32). Jesus' reply indicates that He condemned such lustful behavior because it cheapens sex and makes it much less than what it was created to be; it denies relationship; and it turns the other person into an object—a thing or a nonperson.[10]

The apostle Paul also strongly asserted that we should "honour marriage and guard the sacredness of sexual intimacy between wife and husband" (Hebrews 13:3, *THE MESSAGE*). He never once inferred or suggested that sex was evil or that a sexually active marital relationship was forbidden. In fact, Paul clearly encouraged married couples to honor the sanctity and holiness of their relationship by enjoying sex as a meaningful part of their marriage. It was something they owed to each other and something that should not be withheld except in temporary circumstances by mutual agreement.

> Is it a good thing to have sexual relations? Certainly—but only within a certain context. It is good for a man to have a wife and for a wife to have a husband. Sexual drives are strong, but marriage is strong enough to contain them and provide for a balanced and fulfilling sexual life in a world of sexual disorder. The marriage bed must be a place of mutuality—the husband seeking to satisfy his wife, the wife seeking to satisfy her husband...abstaining from sex is permissible for a period of time if you both agree to it, and if it is for the purpose of prayer and fasting—but only for such times. Then come back together again. (1 Corinthians 7:1-5, *THE MESSAGE.*)

Paul warned couples against allowing lust to infect their relationship so that their partner became simply an object for sexual gratification—and encouraged them to learn how to control their own body in a way that was holy and honorable (1 Thessalonians 4:4, NIV). He further recognized that sexual union for Christian couples involves both a responsibility and a commitment to remain true and faithful to each other and to maintaining their relationship. This is why Paul was so strongly opposed to a casual sexual relationship. For him, to be involved in such sexual encounters without any emotional involvement was dishonorable and sinful because it violated personhood. Sex always involves feelings and emotions and elicits deep-seated attitudes about ourselves and our partner.

> There is more to sex than mere skin on skin. Sex is as much spiritual mystery as physical fact. As written in Scripture, "the two became one." Since we want to be spiritually one with the Master, we must not pursue the kind of sex that avoids commitment and intimacy, leaving us more lonely than ever— the kind of sex that can never "become one." There is a sense in which sexual sins are different from all others. In sexual sin we violate the sacredness of our own bodies...that were

made for...God-modeled love, for "becoming one" with another. (1 Corinthians 6:16-18, *THE MESSAGE.*)

Surely, the tragedy of history is that the church has so often ignored the unashamed eroticism of the creation story and the sensual joy of the Song of Solomon.[11] How sad it is that the affirmation of our sexuality by Jesus and Paul has been twisted and debased in ways that have led so many of us to deny or distort this most precious and wonderful God-given gift.

The Function of Marital Sex

What function or purpose does sex fulfill within the marital relationship? From earliest times the three basic purposes of sexuality were seen as:

1. Emotional support and spiritual fulfilment. The sexual act can be a way of both celebrating and strengthening the emotional bond between two married partners. When God instituted marriage as an "order of creation," He gave men and women the means by which love and sexuality can be consummated fully and freely. The consummation of human love through sexual encounter symbolizes "the meeting of persons"; the emotional support gained through the giving and receiving of love and affection; and the joining of human sexuality with personhood, in a way that no other human experience does. Achieving emotional support and spiritual connection is made possible only as couples communicate directly with each other. Genesis 2:18-25 speaks of this consummation of human love as "becoming one flesh"—a unity that involves the total self (sexual, emotional, and spiritual). The apostle Paul refers to it as a "profound spiritual mystery" (Ephesians 5:32).

2. A source of joy and physical pleasure. Sexual desire is a gracious endowment of God—a glorious gift for man's delight and sanctification. It is not improper, nor is it a matter for embarrassed apology. However, sexual desire is recognized as legitimate only when it is subordinated to and controlled by love. According to Jesus, it needs to be disciplined and directed (Matthew 25:27, 28) through an attitude of responsibility and respect.

For those who tend to devalue the sexual experience, the Song of Solomon, in particular, provides abundant evidence that God's blessing rests on the husband and wife who experience the sheer delight that accompanies the sensual pleasures of lovemaking and who warmly respond to the erotic aspects of their sexual lives together. It is in fact difficult to read the Song of Solomon without coming to the conclusion that God intended the sexual encounter to be "a gloriously sensual and erotic experience"—a genuine celebration of the love relationship.

3. The procreation and nurture of children. Sexual love is also the process through which the human race creatively reproduces itself and takes responsibility for the care and nurture of its young people. While the animal kingdom has no sex life apart from procreation, the sexual relationship for human beings is not limited to procreation. Humans have a sexual desire that is continuous and therefore must come under the control of the mature individual. Aware of the need for accountability to a world facing hunger and overpopulation, responsible parents use contraception as a legitimate means of limiting family size in order to provide adequate child care, while at the same time allowing for the ongoing fulfilment of normal, God-given sexual needs.

Sexual Intimacy and Spiritual Maturity

Sexuality is a vital, fulfilling, and ego-enhancing part of our being that includes more than just sex. Indeed, it is a complex reality that embodies those feelings, perceptions, and behaviors that we have of ourselves and includes the unique combination of our sex (anatomy and physiology), our gender (identity and role), and our personality (spirituality).[11] Perhaps this explains why talking about sexuality is much more difficult than discussing the biological and anatomical aspects of male and female sex. Sex merely hints at and gives us clues to the real essence of our sexuality.

While sex is a gift given to us by God to be richly enjoyed, it has not always been seen or understood that way, even by committed Christians. Since the fall, human beings have found sex perplexing, explosive, and destructive. What was meant to be a blessing quickly became a burden and a dilemma. Prior to the fall, sex aroused no self-consciousness—the Edenic pair were both naked, but they felt no shame (Genesis 2:25). After the fall, they became painfully aware that they were alienated from themselves, each other, God, and the rest of creation. They had lost connection. Life had become confused and distorted. Their trust was broken; their love overwhelmed by hate and fear; abuse and injustice became a threat to their peace and harmony.

Similarly, our sexuality causes us to experience acutely these very same tensions. Our search for love, our yearning to connect with "the other," our desire to become "one flesh," is so often frustrated by our sense of detachment and disconnectedness. It is only by the grace of Christ that our passions are purified, our desires disciplined and controlled by love, and our humanity fulfilled as we are transformed by the Spirit into the likeness of Christ.

To become "one flesh" does not just involve the body—it is a total experience that engages our body, psyche, and spirit and symbolizes an underlying unity of heart and mind and spirit. You cannot separate "body" from "personhood." That is why sexuality is not just about our desire for personal gratification—it is about our yearning for connectedness and completeness. To sever sexuality from relationship, intimacy, and love—to simply reduce it to something that happens only *to* us and not *between* us—is to miss the heart of what sexuality is really all about.

Michael Frost, in his insightful and provocative book, *Longing for Love*, suggests that "when we seek to gratify ourselves sexually, we are also, perhaps unknowingly, yearning to make basic, core spiritual connections. Because sexuality is about engaging my body; my psyche; my masculinity/femininity; my quest for love, acceptance and security; my desire for pleasure, power and meaning—then it is about a profound spiritual reality."[13] Or, to put it in the words of Emil Brunner, "Our sexuality penetrates to the deepest metaphysical ground of our personality."[14]

Those who fail to make the connection between sexuality and the interpersonal life will no doubt miss the connection between sexuality and spirituality also. When we explore human sexuality, we are really dealing with human spirituality—a desire, a yearning, a deep longing that will satisfy us physically, emotionally, and spiritually. C.S. Lewis once suggested that physical pleasures "are not the thing itself; they are only the scent of a flower we have not found, the echo of a time we have not heard, news from a country we have not visited."[15]

So too, human sexuality is a beautiful and mystical experience that connects us with another reality—a spiritual reality. It constitutes a sign or symbol of our ultimate search for "the other"—our yearning for our ultimate destiny with God. This quest is anchored not just in our bodies but in our psyches and our spirits as well. And the ecstatic experiences that fulfill us physically, emotionally, and psychologically are also echoes that there is more for us—and that we will never be genuinely satisfied or fulfilled until we have connected with "the other" and have encountered the One we truly seek.[16]

Because our sexuality is such a powerful vehicle for connection with "the other," and because it is such an intrinsic part of our spiritual makeup, whenever it becomes damaged, abused, misused, or counterfeited, the repercussions are enormous.[17] When "the person" is concealed in the sexual encounter and one detaches their sexual identity from love and from the other person, they counterfeit the revelation of themselves or their "being" to "the other." The possible consequences for such concealment and alienation from sexuality and the marital relationship results either in one person seeking sexual experiences outside the marriage, or sex within the marriage becomes a physical recreation at best, or a humiliating and devastating travesty of the relationship at worst. This concealment of "personhood" in sexuality results not only in harm to a human partner, but it equally leads to denial and confusion about one's own sexuality. This presuming to conceal one's "person" from "the other" constitutes what scripture calls sin, because it violates the divine command and intention of our sexuality by destroying relationship and connectedness.

The ability to truly connect—to share a deep intimacy of being with another—is what being one flesh really means. Through the intimacy of the sexual encounter, a husband and wife enter into an experience that is both private and personal. It is a medium through which mutual self-disclosure occurs, and the senses become the channel for the communication of all that lies too deep for human speech to utter, yet somehow must be told. It is an experience that is associated with the joyous sense of exhilarating achievement, and an equally joyous sense of total abandonment of the whole self (body, psyche, spirit) into the hands of the one we love. This moment enables us to find our true self and experience the most unselfish moment of human existence. This giving of one's self becomes a moment of supreme generosity, an intimacy that is as complete as it can be, a moment that Karl Barth once described as "a blessed frenzy, a breathtaking dialectic of self fulfilment and self forgetfulness, a sublime fulfilment and a scared ratification of love."[18]

When couples embrace these concepts, they can begin to appreciate just how closely sexual intimacy is connected to spiritual maturity. As they are sexually gratified, both physically and emotionally, so together they grow spiritually as well. Through the bodily stimulation, the sexual excitement, and the intense experience of orgasm, a special moment of closeness occurs that creates a synergy, a sense of *commune*-ity that connects two people to each other, to their thinking, feelings, aspirations and values, in a way that is healing, healthy, and wholesome.

Five Phases of Human Sexual Arousal

Defining and affirming a positive and healthy view of sex and human sexuality has been a critical and necessary part of our journey to discover how sexual intimacy is achieved within marriage. Having explored this aspect of sexuality, we now turn to a brief discussion about the five phases of sexual arousal that men and women experience as they respond to one another during a sexual encounter. An understanding of these phases of arousal and the emotional and biological forces at work in sexuality will help clear up many of the issues that concern married couples in their sexual relationship with each other. It will also enable us to take further steps toward dispelling those myths and misconceptions that create barriers to attaining greater intimacy in marriage.

Our awareness of the physiological aspects of sexual arousal were carefully detailed in *Human Sexual Response,* which was first published in 1966 by William Masters and Virginia Johnson. Their classic research findings indicated that the human sexual response cycle is a natural biologic function described by four stages of arousal:

1. Excitement.
2. Plateau.
3. Orgasm.
4. Resolution.

Though arbitrarily defined, these stages correspond to varying levels of sexual arousal and describe the typical responses people have during sexual function. They are not simply mechanical processes detached from thoughts or feelings but are part of the whole sexual involvement and identity of the whole person.[19]

A decade later, Helen Singer Kaplan, in *The New Sex Therapy,* suggested a triphasic concept of human sexuality—Desire, Excitement, and Orgasm. What she proposed essentially was that a "Desire" phase be added to our existing understanding of sexual response. (She actually collapsed the four stages of Masters and Johnson's work into two—excitement and orgasm—believing that the resolution stage merely reflected the absence of sexual arousal.) These three phases, she saw as physiologically related and interconnected but discrete and more accurate for dealing with inhibitions and disorders at each phase.[20] This addition to our understanding about sexual responses has helped considerably in recent times, as couples struggle to come to terms with the differences in their levels of desire or sex drive.

If couples know about these five phases of sexual arousal, there is a much greater probability that they will have no difficulty in their sexual adjustment. Awareness of the physiological, psychological, and emotional responses associated with each of these phases is helpful. It enables a couple to anticipate more accurately their responses and synchronize their expectations in order to achieve greater fulfilment and harmony. While it is true that the various phases of sexual response follow a consistent pattern of progression, the degree to which female and male response patterns may actually vary is considerable. (See Figure 6.) However, it needs to be understood that the strength and speed of the sexual response does not equate with the level of gratification a person experiences or the proficiency of their partner. The degree to which one's sexual experience is better than another depends entirely on an individual's perspective and level of satisfaction.

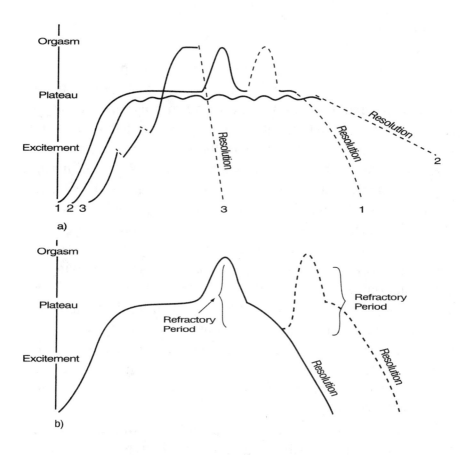

Figure 6: The Human Sexual Response Cycle

The first figure shows three representative variations of the female sexual response.
The second figure shows the most typical pattern for male sexual response.
Source: William Masters and Virginia Johnson, *Human Sexual Response*, 1996.

1. Desire phase. Sexual desire or libido refers to the way an individual is motivated to seek out or become receptive to sexual experiences. The level of desire can range from "too much," to "too little," or none at all. Unfortunately, our understanding of desire is colored by our current social attitudes toward sex. The present obsession with sex suggests that high levels of desire, manifest by frequent sexual thoughts and fantasies and an awareness of feeling "horny," should be regarded as normal and desirable. Low levels of libido are regarded as abnormal or inadequate. Some conservative Christians see low libido as a sign that a person is godly and chaste—and those with "too much" desire as victims of a lust they can barely control.

Couples need to be educated about the true nature of sexual desire. They need to learn how to handle the anxiety and excesses that are prevalent in our sex-saturated society, that presumes and demands that "normal" people are the ones who enjoy sex, look forward to it with positive anticipation, and have a high sex drive. Much of the hype around issues of desire can therefore cause marital partners to bicker and fight as they become angry, frustrated, and disappointed over questions such as, "How often should we have sex?" " Is my partner's sex drive normal?" "Are we sexually compatible?" "How do we deal with discrepancies in desire?" or "Is my sex drive normal?"

Because married couples tend to become anxious and concerned about the differences in their sex drives, they need to know some of the following facts about desire. First, differences in sex drive are an inevitability in all healthy, long-term relationships. It is ridiculous to expect sexual synchronicity and erotic harmony, with sex drives in perfect tune. Discrepancies in desire are a normal part of long-term relationships. Couples need to know that desire ebbs and flows throughout the life of a relationship and that it is enhanced or inhibited by a range of hormonal, physical, emotional, cognitive, relational, and situational factors. A woman's desire is enhanced by social acceptability—such as a happy relationship, relaxation and contentment, normal hormone levels, physical well-being, a positive attitude to sex, and adequate privacy. A man's desire is enhanced by visual stimulation. For a list of inhibitors to sexual desire, see Table 5 (facing page). Inhibitors need to be minimized and enhancers maximized.

Furthermore, those who initiate lovemaking tend to manifest higher desire. Those who never initiate lovemaking may be quite receptive to sex and still manifest a healthy sex drive. It also needs to be recognized that the difference in sex drive between men and women is not in quantity but in quality. Female sex drive is more distractible. It is more easily turned off by the vicissitudes of life and love. Men's sex drive is more urgent, less distractible, and more focused on intercourse and orgasm.

Given the right frame of mind and the right conditions, couples can enjoy sex without first having desire, but it doesn't matter how often they make love, so long as both partners are happy about the frequency. Research shows that desire tends to be significantly influenced by changes in hormone levels in both men and women.

A person with low levels of desire will need more time, more energy, and more stimulation to experience arousal and orgasm should they choose to get "turned on." Frequently, a partner with high desire can end up "labeling" the partner with a lower desire for sex with all kinds of derogatory labels and ends up coming across as over-demanding, unreasonable, and overbearing. Discrepancies in desire can set up a negative cycle in which the higher-drive partner constantly *pursues* the lower-drive partner, who becomes the *distancer*. This cycle results in a lot of blaming, frustration, and anger and needs to be interrupted and stopped.

Finally, couples need to know that sexual compatibility involves accepting differences in levels of desire, working at meeting each other's needs, and striving for emotional and sexual harmony. To achieve compatability, it is very important to create partner empathy. You cannot have good sex in a bad relationship.

2. Excitement phase. The Excitement phase is different from the desire phase but is linked to it in the sense that an interest in or desire for sex makes it easier to be aroused. It is initiated in response to certain stimuli to the senses, with touching being a most

Physical

- Fatigue
- Pain (headache, backache, arthritis, painful intercourse)
- Feeling unwell, nausea
- Poor health
- Chronic illness
- Some medications
- Hormonal changes
- Breastfeeding
- Menopause

Psychological

- Lack of emotional well-being—stress, guilt, anger, worry, resentment, sadness, frustration, depression, shame
- Poor self-esteem
- Feelings of sexual inadequacy
- Poor sex education
- Negative sexual attitudes
- Poor body image
- Lack of pleasurable sexual thoughts and fantasies

Relationship

- Love attraction
- Sexual difficulties
- Limited sensuality
- Lack of affection, companionship
- Fun and romance
- Lack of trust
- Unresolved jealousy
- Insecurity—lack of commitment
- Poor communication
- Lack of intimacy
- Lack of respect
- Boundary intrusions, e.g.: work demands, in-laws, children, social activities, hobbies

Situational

- Lack of privacy
- Poor atmosphere in lovemaking, e.g.: lack of time, distractions from kids, TV, phone

Table 5: List of Inhibitors

important avenue for experiencing arousal. Some areas of the body have a richer supply of nerve endings, so greater arousal is possible. Other senses such as vision, hearing, smell, and taste are to a lesser extent a means of stimulation.

Physical stimulation alone, however, is not sufficient for a satisfying, long-term sexual relationship. Arousal is also enhanced by emotional states, which include feeling cherished, trusted, and respected. Mental or physical distractions, or feelings such as anxiety, hostility, and devaluation can significantly block off response patterns.

Couples need to appreciate that arousal during the excitement phase does not occur at the same rate for men and women. Surveys indicate that a woman in the first stage of love-play needs between twenty and forty minutes to achieve complete arousal.[23] Men's arousal, which is linked more to visual stimulation, often requires as little as one to five minutes in time. Such a discrepancy in arousal during this phase can lead to a lot of misunderstanding and frustration if partners do not pay attention to each other's love-play needs. When men try to rush through love-play in order to get to intercourse and orgasm before a woman is ready, it often causes frustration, resentment, and pain. Men need to remember that a woman's arousal is more emotional than physical, and it tends to be diffused over the whole body so that touch, stimulation, and love-play are vital to good arousal.

3. Plateau phase. During this phase, many of the physiological and emotional processes which began in the excitement phase are now carried to their conclusion. Kaplan saw the excitement and plateau phases as the same, and while the transition point is not clear-cut, the distinct emphasis in the plateau phase is the necessary time lapse which should exist between excitement and orgasm. This is the time for love-play—a time to savor each passing moment in a state of heightened arousal. (You will notice that we refer to love-play, not foreplay. Foreplay tends to put the focus on orgasm as "the main event" and devalues the repertoire of lovemaking activities that are an essential part of the enjoyment, pleasure, and complete arousal that climaxes in orgasm.)

The plateau stage is usually the longest of the four phases of arousal and should not be rushed. Men, in particular, have a tendency to ignore the value of this phase and fail to acknowledge that women deeply appreciate the opportunity to enjoy the teasing and the touching, the playfulness and the pleasuring, the communication and the emotional intensity, experienced during love play. Failure to enjoy the love-play of this phase can lead a woman to experience feelings of deep resentment that their partner sees them only as an object for self-gratification. Some men complain that they receive messages from their partner to "hurry up and get it over with" as the reason for their not prolonging love-play. In these cases, couples may need to review their attitude, if this contributes to feelings of disconnection.

4. Orgasm phase. This is seen as the culmination of complete sexual arousal. This consummate moment is the shortest phase of the response cycle and is full of physical and emotional intensity. It is a special gift that God has given for humans to enjoy. He designed that this moment—this act of one-fleshness—would bring together two committed people in a throb of unity and connectedness, a union designed to be the means of bonding a man and a woman together in pleasure, potential, and praise.[24]

At the time of orgasm, the body releases a neurohormone called oxytocin, which not only triggers the orgasm but induces a feeling of safety, security, and tender empathy. Oxytocin, which is sometimes referred to as the "snuggle hormone," is the neurochemical of intimate connection. It promotes intense closeness, trust, and attachment behaviors and is the same hormone that is secreted when a mother is breast-feeding her baby.[25]

Couples need to understand that the orgasmic phase of their sexual experience is not a goal to achieve but an experience to enjoy. There is far too much emphasis today placed on performance and technique, which only turns lovemaking into a competitive experience with a focus on "turning your partner wild in bed." These attitudes tend to divert attention away from the joy and satisfaction that comes from celebrating the relationship and results in the devaluation and desecration of that special moment.

118 • SEARCHING FOR INTIMACY IN MARRIAGE

Concepts such as "achieve," "attain," or "reach," when speaking about orgasm, make it sound as if this is the whole and only focus of lovemaking.

For most women, sexual intercourse can be ruined if orgasm is the goal. It needs to be remembered that a woman can be "turned on" sexually and enjoy the sexual experience and not have an orgasm. In fact, researchers say that 50 percent of sexually active women do not achieve orgasm every time they have intercourse and that they do not need to experience orgasm every time to enjoy sex.

Furthermore, the emphasis in the media on the need for couples to strive for simultaneous orgasms—or for women to achieve multiple orgasmic experiences—is only further evidence for this focus on performance. It is fortunate that simultaneous orgasms are no longer considered a hallmark of mature sexuality. Researchers point out just how difficult this is for couples to achieve, given the many cultural and individual differences that influence male and female sexual responses. Many partners feel that their enjoyment is doubled when they attend to their own pleasure in a separate moment and then focus on being aware of their partner's rapture.[26]

5. Resolution phase. The sexual experience is still not complete once orgasm has been consummated. This final phase is a time when arousal subsides and couples have a chance to prolong the experience and savor the profound feelings of emotional closeness and connection. This phase is sometimes referred to as the "afterglow experience" and is especially relished by women. When men skip this afterglow time, women often interpret their behavior as switching off emotionally and feel betrayed by the fact that their lovemaking has been reduced to a purely mechanical experience devoid of emotional connection.

Couples need to appreciate that "resolution" is a good time to continue verbal and tactile communication as a way of affirming and celebrating the special gifts they share together. Men especially need to recognize how much women desire closeness and intimacy in relationship and how their lack of caressing, cuddling, and touching—and their withdrawal during the resolution phase—can cause resentment and reductions in desire. Women who do react negatively at this stage of the sexual experience may in fact be trying, passively, to redress the insensitivity of their partners or the imbalance of power in the relationship.

Achieving Sexual Satisfaction

Couples quickly come to realize that the quality of their sexual relationship influences how they feel about themselves, each other, and the level of satisfaction they enjoy within their marriage. Achieving a fulfilling sex life is not something that just happens—it takes a lot of emotional investment, and it requires a great amount of understanding, acceptance, and adjustment on the part of two people. Outlined below are six important qualities for developing and maintaining a healthy and satisfying sexual relationship.

1. A clear focus. The sexual experience is all about achieving mutual satisfaction and a deep sense of personal closeness. It is not about performance or technique. Sexual techniques don't resolve difficulties with sex and intimacy. Sexual enjoyment is far more complex than simply the physical meeting of persons. Performance only tends to generate anxiety, and the greater the anxiety, the greater the possibility of failure and feeling inadequate. No, sex is meant to be enjoyable, satisfying, and fun. The emphasis here is on experiencing, not performing.

2. A positive attitude. Negative attitudes toward sex create barriers that frustrate and distance two people from each other. Sex needs to be rescued from faulty attitudes and feelings of inadequacy.[27] Lori Gordon suggests that there are four main enemies to developing a satisfying sexual relationship. They are:

a. *Lack of time and failure to schedule pleasure into our lives—* a healthy sex life requires scheduled time and energy.

b. *One or both partners' lack of desire or an imbalance between frequency of desire*—which may have roots in emotional needs. Such things as chronic stress, overcommitment, indifference, mistrust, boredom, lingering anger, resentment, guilt, and shame can seriously undermine sexual desire. Desire may also be inhibited by fears of pregnancy, infertility, being punished, or simply embarrassed by being unattractive or unacceptable.

c. *The misuse of sex*—where sex is used to coerce, manipulate, or exploit another person. It can be used as a substitute for bonding and affection, a leverage for getting what one wants, or it can be withheld in order to avoid feelings of being controlled.

d. *Ignorance and misinformation*—which are often reinforced by the belief that talking about sex robs it of its spontaneity and romance. Unreal expectations or naiveté can impact sexual desire in significant ways.

3. Adequate knowledge. Satisfied couples demonstrate a good knowledge of the five phases of sexual arousal and understand the basic differences in desire between men and women. They recognize that sex drives vary and that love-play and adequate stimulation are required to enjoy good sex. They also recognize that both partners need to be fully involved in the sexual process for the pleasure and enjoyment of it, not just for the result. They do not see a failure to reach orgasm as a sign of failure—rather, they focus on listening, understanding, and connecting with the desires and emotional needs of their partner. Satisfied couples enjoy a sense of reciprocity in lovemaking, in which each feels free to initiate sex or enjoy being receptive to their partner's advances.

4. Accept responsibility. Couples who enjoy a satisfying sexual relationship do not hold the view that one partner is responsible for the fulfillment of the other. They accept that their primary responsibility is to take care of themselves and ask for what they want or need. They accept that their happiness, satisfaction, or disappointment is very much related to their own behavior and attitudes.

5. Communicate desire. Developing a good sexual relationship depends vitally on good communication. Lovemaking's main function is to create a mutual bond based on pleasure-giving, positive talk, thoughtfulness, consideration, playfulness, gentle touching, nonjudgmental support, and the anticipation of the other's needs. Couples who learn to talk freely and openly about their feelings and sexual responses tend to establish a greater sense of understanding and closeness. Issues of desire and any discrepancies they may experience can be talked over without fear or threat of reprisal. The best sex occurs when partners have learned to be comfortable with their own and their partner's sexuality. When this happens, their feelings grow deeper, and sexual desire occurs more frequently. As the process of communication develops a sense of comfortableness between the couple, the special ingredient of playfulness begins to blossom. Sexual satisfaction builds as both parties know that their individual uniqueness is valued, respected, and cherished. They feel safe with each other, and the desire for closeness and intimacy grows. Through a combination of friendship, trust, and playfulness, love and passion are kept alive, and romance flourishes in the relationship.

6. Enjoy mutuality. Mutuality assumes that there is a mutual desire for and interest in lovemaking and that sexual harmony is achieved by couples through effective verbal communication and a sensitive understanding of each other's needs. It suggests that married partners allow their natural feelings, inclinations, and actions to occur without a conscious evaluation of the performance. There is no game playing or hiding one's true feelings and desires during the sexual encounter.[28] The sexual relationship is therefore kept alive and vital because of the mutual involvement, enjoyment, and responsibility of each partner. Effective sexual love in marriage is found most frequently when both husband and wife willingly focus on expressing and demonstrating love to their partner as well as being open to receiving the love and emotional support they get in return. Mutuality is built around affection, respect, passion, and caring for the other person.

Notes:

1. Diana S. Garland and David E. Garland, *Beyond Companionship* (Philadelphia: Westminster Press, 1986), p. 136.

2. Stanley Keleman, *In Defense of Heterosexuality* (Berkeley: Center Press, 1982), pp. 15, 18, 19.

3. William Masters, Virginia Johnson, and Robert Kolodny, *Human Sexuality* (Boston: Little Brown & Company, 1982)

4. Oscar Feucht, ed., *Sex and the Church* (St Louis: Concordia Publishing House, 1961), p. 57.

5. Ibid.

6. Ibid., p. 72.

7. Ibid., p. 122, 123.

8. Stuart Barton Babbage, *Sex and Sanity* (London: Hodder and Stoughton, 1965), p. 19.

9. Richard Foster, *Money, Sex and Power* (London: Hodder and Stoughton, 1985), pp. 95-98.

10. Ibid., pp. 98, 99.

11. Ibid., p. 101.

12. Michael Frost, *Longing for Love* (Sydney: Albatross Books,1996), p. 32.

13. Ibid., pp. 19, 22.

14. Emil Brunner, *The Christian Doctrine of Creation and Redemption* (London: Lutterworth Press, 1964), p. 63.

15. C.S. Lewis, quoted in *A Cloud of Witnesses*, by Alister McGrath (Leicester: Intervarsity Press, 1990), p. 127.

16. Michael Frost, *Longing for Love*, pp. 23-25.

17. Ibid., p. 34.

18. Stuart Barton Babbage, *Sex and Sanity,* p. 27.

19. William Masters, Virginia Johnson, and Robert Kolodny, *Human Sexuality,* p. 57.

20. Helen Singer Kaplan, *Disorders of Sexual Desire* (New York: Brunner/Mazel, 1979), pp. 5, 6.

21. Rosie McInnes, "A Practical Approach to Desire Problems." *Psychotherapy in Australia,* vol. 3, May 1997, pp. 28-33.

22. Ibid.

23. Alberta Mazat, *Capitivated By Love* (Mountain View, Calif.: Pacific Press Publishing Association, 1986), p. 44.

24. Ibid., p. 41.

25. Jon Carlson and Len Sperry, *The Intimate Couple* (Philadelphia: Brunner/Mazel, 1999), p. 62.

26. Alberta Mazat, *Capitivated By Love*, p. 47.

27. Lori H. Gordon, *Passage to Intimacy* (New York: Simon and Schuster, 1993), pp. 250, 251.

28. Jack O. Balswick and Judith K. Balswick, *The Family* (Michigan: Baker Book House, 1991), pp. 189-193.

FIVE

Marital Conflict

A marriage relationship is never static—it is constantly changing. As couples journey together, they seek, through the process of mutual influence, to get to know one another better, to
accommodate one another as they face incompatibilities and differences, and to develop a sense of closeness and emotional connection. However, the feeling of closeness soon disappears, and
understanding goes out the window when they stop listening to
each other, because one or both of them feels ignored, misunderstood, or under emotional attack by their partner.

Current research clearly shows that the greatest obstacle to
achieving intimacy and satisfaction in marriage is a couple's inability to handle successfully their conflicts and disagreements. It
is not how much they love each other, how great their sex life is,
or even how they deal with their money or discipline their kids
that best predicts the quality of their relationship—it is the way
they deal with their differences.[1] Virginia Satir believed that individuals cannot be real or develop a truly human and zestful relationship with one another until they have confronted and successfully handled their differentness.[2] Being able to deal with
"differentness," which covers the whole range of individual differences, is what constitutes the core experience of every successful marriage.

John Gottman summed up the last twenty years of his research on marriage by saying:

> The one lesson I have learned from my years of research is that a lasting marriage results from a couple's ability to resolve the conflicts that are inevitable in any relationship. Many couples tend to equate a low level of conflict with happiness and believe the claim "we never fight" is a sign of health. But I believe we grow in our relationships by reconciling our differences. That is how we become more loving people and truly experience the fruits of marriage.[3]

It is important to recognize that what Gottman is saying is that couples come to know each other more intimately by *reconciling* their differences. He is not suggesting that marriage is about *resolving* or neutralizing differences but about how well married partners learn to live together in spite of their inherent differences. What matters most is the way they handle the inevitable differences that arise whenever two people form a partnership. Which raises the question, "Why is it that dealing with our differences is so difficult?"

The Role of Emotion in Marital Conflict

Based on the work of John Gottman and a number of other marital researchers, the causes of unhappiness and distress in marriage are no longer a mystery. Their research has clearly shown that the nature of marital distress is related to the way couples deal with their differentness and reconcile the problems that develop within their marriage as one or both of them feel: (a) *flooded* by negative emotions, and (b) *trapped* in narrow, negative interactional patterns that constrict and contain conflict and regulate feelings of fear and rejection.[4]

These two key findings focus our attention on the need to acknowledge the compelling role that emotion plays in marital disagreements and the distress it creates among couples as they try to resolve their difference. These findings also highlight the need for us to address explicitly the importance of the emotional bond that exists between two married people and the interactional process of attachment by which it is formed. Feelings of vulnerability, insecurity, and abandonment—and the damage done to the marriage relationship by ongoing unresolved conflict—can only be addressed and repaired as attention is given to developing those attachment behaviors that rebuild and strengthen the emotional bond between the couple.

How emotions are dealt with in a marriage relationship is crucial. Many difficulties in marriage have their genesis in the way couples process their feelings with each other or the way they respond negatively to expressions of emotion. Problems often arise when married partners fail in accurately reading one another's emotions—or when they attempt to avoid or control the expression of feelings within the relationship. This tends to foster cycles of negative interaction and create misunderstandings and distress that result either in hostility, defensiveness, or withdrawal.[5]

Central to the issue of marital conflict is the degree to which couples feel vulnerable to each other or afraid that their partner will not understand how they feel or will not emotionally support them. The fear of being attacked, abandoned, rejected, or simply found to be incompetent or inadequate tends not only to restrict the way in which information is shared or processed but to evoke behaviors that ultimately put the marriage at risk. When feelings of frustration, fear, anger, and hurt remain after an intense emotional exchange has occurred, a partner can often be left brooding over his or her wounds and contemplating the future state of the relationship. Such feelings only inhibit the growth of trust and intimacy and prevent the development of any meaningful connection.

When couples are reactive to each other and find it difficult to process their emotional reactions, the second major issue emerges. In their attempt to deal with the fear of being misunderstood or rejected, married partners generate heightened feelings of anxiety and insecurity. Many see this anxiety as an attachment issue, which fosters the establishment of recurring cycles of negative interaction designed to reestablish connection by inviting or demanding that the other partner becomes more accessible and responsive. If this does not happen, the pursuing partner intensifies efforts— through behaviors that lead either to protesting, clinging, or simply avoiding or withdrawing from the other partner—until they become more available and responsive and reestablish meaningful contact.

These negative, repetitive cycles of interaction are maintained by compelling emotional exchanges that take on a life of their own as married partners critically attack, condemn, blame, and even show contempt toward each other. This negativity, which begins to pervade the whole relationship, can often result in the development of a most common interactional pattern called the "Attack-Withdraw Pattern," in which pursuit on the part of one partner is reciprocated with distancing by the other. When a couple fails to find ways to deal with these negative forces and build positive connections with each other, respect and goodwill begin to disappear from the marriage, and the relationship really struggles to survive.[7]

According to Gottman, what really separates contented couples from those in deep misery is the way they successfully establish a healthy balance between the positive and negative feelings and actions that they express toward each other. The couple's negative feelings and frequent arguments are balanced with lots of love and compassion; lots of empathy and affirmation; and plenty of touching, smiling, and laughing. The predominance of these positive behaviors in their marriage acts as a nutrient, nurturing the affection, joy, and contentment that strengthens the couple's ability to deal with their differences and weather the rough storms of conflict and disagreement.

Interestingly, Gottman further acknowledges that negativity and conflict serve a very positive function in a marriage by facilitating the cycle of closeness and distance which actually creates the dynamic that prevents stagnation and stimulates relational renewal and intimacy. He suggests a certain amount of negativity may be required to foster creativity in the marriage and help it to thrive.

But while that may be true, one thing is quite clear: Too much negativity is definitely destructive to the relationship.[8]

Defining Conflict

Robert Bolton says that "you cannot find personal intimacy without conflict. Love and conflict are inseparable."[9] That may be true! However, even though conflict may be a normal, unavoidable part of our relationships, it is not something we seek or enjoy. Most of us find conflict disruptive and destructive, and we will do anything to avoid it, even to the point of suppressing our feelings and emotional reactions when we are confronted, challenged, or frustrated.

The scriptures warn us about the destructive effect that negative behaviors and conflict can have in our relationship. The wise man Solomon said that "gentle words bring life and health; a deceitful tongue crushes the spirit" (Proverbs 15:4, NLT). He instructed us to remember that "beginning a quarrel is like opening a floodgate, so drop the matter before a dispute breaks out" (Proverbs 17:14, NLT).

The apostle Paul urged two individuals at Philippi to "iron out their differences and make up. God does not want his children holding grudges" (Philippians 4:1, *THE MESSAGE*). He also wrote a long letter to the believers at Ephesus, counseling them not to "let any unwholesome talk come out of your mouths, but only what is helpful for building others up according to their needs...and get rid of all bitterness, rage and anger, brawling and slander...be kind and compassionate to one another, forgiving each other just as in Christ God forgave you" (Ephesians 4:29, 31, NIV).

Peterson defines conflict as "an interpersonal process that occurs whenever the actions of one person interfere with the actions of another." Newton Malony sees conflict as a fight for life. He proposes that we make a clear distinction between conflict and problems, because, as he says, "conflict" is really about our inner response to those external threats that endanger our status, identity, and self-esteem. When our self-esteem suffers a real or imaginary blow, we are forced to defend ourselves or be psychologically devastated. The term *problem,* he applies to those situations that involve disputes or differences of opinion between two individuals or groups of people[11]—a struggle over goals or values.

The Basic Components of Conflict

These distinctions are useful, because they serve to remind us that there are two basic components to conflict:

1. The emotional component. This constitutes the relational dimension, which includes feelings of anger, distrust, defensiveness, scorn, resentment, fear, and rejection.

2. The specific issues component. This aspect of conflict involves conflicting needs and values, disagreements over policies and practices, and differing conceptions of roles and uses of resources. These two components are often intertwined and difficult to separate.[12] The specific issues frequently generate emotional conflict, and the emotional component can tend to multiply the specific issues.

In this regard, two guiding principles generally apply when one is dealing with these two components of conflict. First, if the relationship is spontaneous and healthy, the emotional or relational aspect tends to recede into the background. Second, the more one struggles to define or acknowledge the emotional component, the less importance they attach to the special issues or content aspect of the conflict.

Consequently, when couples deal with the conflict that emerges in their relationship, they need to be encouraged to identify these two components and *deal constructively with the emotional component first.*

When the adrenaline is flowing and the emotions are aroused, married partners are more volatile and ready for combat, so it is important that they learn to listen and connect first with each others feelings. Nothing will get resolved until they first connect with the frustration and hurt that motivates the anger being expressed either verbally or nonverbally.

Deal with specific issues second. The ability to calmly and rationally examine the specific issues creating the dispute is frequently impossible in the early stages of an argument or disagreement. Couples need to connect first with the feelings; then seek to rationally resolve the problem.

In marital conflict, the specific issues or problems that arise can be divided into two categories:

1. Solvable problems. Even though problems can cause excessive tension, many of them are resolved by the couple. When there is no underlying feeling that fuels the dispute, and they are able to validate each other's feelings and perspectives, they can quickly come to some compromise or resolution. If, however, "they don't work to find a compromise on the issue, it is likely that they will become increasingly resentful and entrenched in their positions. The conflict could deepen and take on more symbolic meaning. In other words, it could evolve into a grid locked, perpetual problem."[13]

2. Perpetual problems. Seventy percent of marital conflict falls into this category. Instead of coping with problems effectively, the couple gets "gridlocked" over them. They find themselves going over and over the same ground time and time again, yet their arguments never resolve anything. They become more and more entrenched in their positions and gradually begin to feel psychologically overwhelmed. The couple then begin the process of gradually disengaging themselves emotionally from each other.[14]

A number of significant factors can influence the way a couple goes about dealing with their problems and resolving specific issues. Some married partners are fortunate that they have a great similarity in attitudes, interests, and personalities. This gives them much more common ground either to tolerate or work out their differences. However, in relationships where one of the partners is neurotic, there is a greater likelihood that this partner will overreact emotionally to conflicts of interest and use coercion, avoidance, and escalation to deal with problems. In other cases, marital partners may have differing levels of conflict resolution skills or a different capacity for tolerating or handling stress. These differences can affect the way they deal with and resolve their differences. Stress, in particular, is likely to increase a partner's need for support, while simultaneously decreasing the ability to provide support.[15]

Sources of Conflict in Marriage

A number of issues exist that typically create conflict for marital couples. However, the nature of these issues tends to change in importance and intensity as the couple passes through the various stages of the family life cycle and journey toward relational maturity. The quality of their relationship very much depends on how they deal with frustrating events, daily demands, and differences of opinion that emerge to impact their relationship.

Most of the research on marital conflict reveals that there are three main issues that married couples consistently fight about: money, sex, and communication. Many couples find these issues the most difficult to deal with, because they are symptomatic of fundamental core issues in the marriage relationship that relate to their survival, emotional security, and intimacy. They represent specific issues that are regularly encountered, and some agreement is needed on how they will be dealt with and managed, if the relationship is to function effectively.

Couples who seek marriage counseling initially say the major problem between them is that they "just can't communicate" with each other. Poor communication is a common cause of conflict and disagreement, and it happens when partners find it difficult to express their needs, wants, and feelings—or when they resort constantly to questioning, criticizing, or condemning their partner. If couples fail to share ideas, opinions, and general information with each other, this often leaves them feeling isolated, ignored, and emotionally unsupported. When this happens, they typically end up pursuing each other and engaging in bickering and fighting.

Some of the other common issues of conflict—beside money, sex, and communication—are related to relationship and family matters. Couples typically fight about the lack of agreed leadership in the relationship and who is responsible for making the final decisions, unequal distribution of housework, and failure to complete assigned household chores. Family issues are more about the discipline and nurturing of the children, establishing and maintaining appropriate boundaries with in-laws and extended family members, and how to balance work and family responsibilities.

At a deeper level, the source of marital conflict is frequently found in the personality or gender differences that exist between the married partners—or the degree to which their family backgrounds influence and create disagreements. A wide range of personality differences can irritate and frustrate couples, causing them unconsciously to gripe and complain to the partner about unreasonable expectations or demands that pressure the relationship. Differences such as neatness, punctuality, self-discipline, ambition, energy levels, dominance, jealousy, lack of generosity, the need for excitement or relaxation, negativity, or a lack of assertiveness—to mention just a few—can easily become wonderful grist for the mill of discontent, irritation, and disputation.

Gender differences can also cause personal friction and conflict to occur within the marriage relationship. Discrepancies in sexual desire (chapter 4) and differences in the way men and women approach relationships and communication (chapter 2) have already been discussed. However, some further interesting research findings show how husbands tend to withdraw from conflict because of the unpleasantness of their physiological arousal during arguments, whereas wives tend to raise the intensity and escalate the conflict when they sense their husband's nonresponsiveness and avoidant behavior. Men tend to be "too rational" and downplay emotions during conflict, whereas women are more likely to complain and criticize.[16] Because men and women tend to have two very different ways of expressing and experiencing emotion, this too can create a lot of misunderstanding and disagreement within the marriage relationship.[17]

Differences in family history and background are another major source of conflict and disagreement in marriage which are not often recognized. Couples bring to the marriage relationship a variety of attitudes, values, and beliefs about money (its importance and how it should be managed), sex (its value and function), religion (its central role in the family), and children (how they should be raised—whether strict or lenient) that influence the way they connect and interact with each other as parents and as husband and wife. Differences in these areas, often unspoken and sometimes unacknowledged, can cause huge disagreements. Attitudes toward conflict, anger management, and how to tolerate and deal with stress—learned in their family of origin as they were growing up—often cause a lot of bitter disagreement as the couple becomes frustrated over their mismatched scripts.

Over time, people come to recognize how these issues are the source of their conflict and distress. However, a number of hidden issues often drive the really difficult and destructive arguments. By "hidden," we mean that they are not usually talked about or openly acknowledged.

Markman, et al., describes six types of hidden issues that frequently occur in marital disputes.

1. The issue of power. Couples often unconsciously fight over who has control of the relationship—who has the final say. Constantly, they become caught up in a power struggle to determine the outcome and resolution to issues of concern. Control issues are least likely to damage the relationship when a couple feels that they are a team and that each partner's needs and desires are considered in the decisions that are made.

2. The issue of feeling loved. Married partners need to feel that they are loved and that their emotional needs are being met. Knowing that they are secure in the relationship and that they are needed and cared for by their partner paves the way for greater connection and more efficient problem solving.

3. The issue of recognition. When couples receive recognition and appreciation from their partner for their accomplishments, they feel valued for who they are and for what they do. This not only prevents relationship burnout but provides them with the confidence to deal with issues openly and effectively.

4. The issue of commitment. It is critical for married partners to feel secure in their relationship. When conflict arises, if an individual feels that their partner may "get up and leave," this creates a lot of anxiety and uncertainty and can emotionally block the pathway to conflict resolution.

5. The issue of integrity. Nothing undermines a couple's ability to deal with their problems and differences more than the feeling that their partner questions their motives or intentions. When an individual feels that they are invalidated, insulted, or that their integrity is questioned, these feelings take precedence over any attempts to resolve specific issues or problems.

6. The issue of acceptance. All couples need to feel that they are both accepted and respected by each other. This issue underlies all other issues. The fear of being rejected or found to be unacceptable sabotages an individual's desire to be invested in serious conflict resolution. Markman sees "acceptance as the most basic hidden issue driving the issues of power, caring, commitment and integrity in arguments."[19]

Destructive Patterns of Interaction

Researchers have found that marriages are likely to be stable and satisfying when husbands and wives express five times more positive feelings to each other than they do negative feelings. Some even believe that just one well-directed negative comment has the ability to wipe out the effect of five positive comments—such is the powerful influence of negativity on a marriage. Stable couples tend to show their positive attitude and involvement by:

a. Being actively interested in what their partner is saying.
b. Showing affection and tenderness.
c. Showing their care and concern for their partner.
d. Being empathic, appreciative, and supportive.
e. Being playful, teasing, and funny.
f. Sharing the joy and excitement of spending good times together.[20]

Such positive emotional interaction is based on goodwill and respect and enables loyalty, love, and trust to develop within the relationship.

When couples fail to generate a sense of positivity in their relationship, they typically find themselves engaging in frequent negative exchanges that can become destructive and toxic to the marriage. Once these negative exchanges are embedded in the relationship, they become established patterns that often lead to emotional detachment and distrust. In fact, these patterns, which couples quickly establish in the first two years of their marriage, become the basis of their "fight style" and remain fairly consistent throughout the life of their relationship[21] unless they are consciously modified because of trauma, ultimatum, or bargaining over developmental changes. Frequently, when couples do reach an impasse and feel deeply disappointed and emotionally exposed to one another, they unconsciously find themselves resorting to the use of tactics that they have learned in childhood. These deeply scripted tactics, which often hide layers of emotional injury—and include wariness, defensiveness, and the ability to critically attack their partner—can become the greatest impediment to the development of marital intimacy.[22]

Worthington suggests that couples that progressively become locked in conflict pass through four stages.[23]

Persuasion. First, they attempt to use their personal power and influence to persuade their partner to accept their point of view. Persuasion is intensified when disagreements are not resolved.

Disagreement over the way the issue is being dealt with and how they are treating each other now becomes the focus of the conflict. Issues of nonacceptance, failure to listen, understanding individual ideas and feelings, and a lack of connection are the dominant concern.

Power strategies. At the third stage, couples begin to use power strategies with each other in order to gain dominance and control. This struggle for control leads to the following:

a. The harder each partner tries, the worse it gets.

b. Each partner focuses on his or her own intentions rather than on the actual consequences of their behavior.

c. Each partner has a dark fantasy of what would happen if they were to change their behavior and break out of the cycle.[24]

These cycles can be highly visible and arouse strong emotional feelings. Some of the common power tactics used during this stage can include threatening, blaming, discounting, withdrawing, belittling, provoking guilt feelings, derailing the discussion, and abandonment.

Personality problems. Core personality issues or differences are blamed as the cause of the problem. So the problem is personalized, with characteristics such as "suspicious," "stubborn," "hostile," or "indifferent" becoming identified as the real issue.

Four Ineffective Ways of Relating

Gottman shows how this downward spiral of interaction draws couples into a free fall toward marital conflict and disharmony, causing their relationship to be consumed with negativity. By recognizing what he calls the "Four Horseman of the Apocalypse,"[25] couples can identify four very ineffective ways of relating to each other than can undermine their communication and signal the beginning of the end of their relationship. In order of the least to the most destructive, these four insidious forces are:

1. Criticism. Expressing differences, seeking to influence each other, or complaining about things that frustrate or offend, are healthy parts of any relationship. However, when couples turn to using criticisms that involve blaming, shaming, or personally accusing and attacking the other person, this becomes very destructive to the relationship.

2. Defensiveness. When marriage partners feel hurt, unappreciated, or unfairly accused, they respond defensively in an effort to protect themselves and ward off the real or perceived attack. Being defensive usually involves responding in ways that deny any responsibility for change, making excuses for actions rather than trying to modify them, cross-complaining and "yes-butting," whining, or constantly repeating back your position to your partner rather than attempting to understand their position.

3. Contempt. When an individual devalues their partner and begins to act in a contemptuous manner by insulting, demeaning, or hurting them, all feelings of intimacy and closeness begin to disappear, and the attacked partner finds it hard to remember any of the other partner's positive qualities. The capacity to respect, affirm, compliment, and support the other person is lost in a flurry of sneering, mockery, and name-calling. Expressing contempt is unquestionably the most corrosive force in marriage.

4. Stonewalling. By emotionally withdrawing and removing oneself from any interaction with their partner, an individual can become a "stonewaller." This act is a very powerful way of conveying one's disapproval, smugness, and icy distance and creating an increase in relational distress. The majority of stonewallers are men, who tend to be more overwhelmed by the emotional arousal of conflict than women.

Only when a marriage eventually turns sour does the ultimate danger of these four destructive forces arise and becomes apparent. As Gottman says:

> What makes the four horsemen so deadly to a marriage is not so much their unpleasantness but the intensive way they interfere with a couple's communication. They create a continuing cycle of discord and negativity that's hard to break through if you don't understand what is happening.[26]

When this stage of discord is finally reached, couples frequently seize their negative thoughts and powerful beliefs about their partner and become locked into feelings of negativity and despair.

This negative inner script is often accompanied by emotional "flooding" that causes an individual to feel so out of control that they become extremely hostile, defensive, or withdrawn as a way of coping with these feelings of overload. If this happens often enough, constructive discussion with their partner becomes impossible, and a chronic shift begins to occurs in the way they think about their partner and their marriage. Vulnerable and reactive, the individual further intensifies the conviction that they will get nowhere by talking things over with their partner, so they take a major step in turning away from the marriage, creating parallel lives, and, with the inevitable outcome of loneliness, disengage from the relationship.[27]

Four Destructive Patterns

Markman, Stanley, and Blumberg have identified four destructive patterns that couples use in communicating with one another, that can successfully sabotage their relationship. These are not the only patterns that lead to marital distress, but they summarize what many studies have revealed as the most potent forces that weaken and even destroy relationships over time.[28]

Escalation occurs when partners respond back and forth negatively to each other, continually upping the ante so conditions get worse and worse. Often, negative comments spiral into increasing anger and frustration. Couples who are happy now and likely to stay that way are less prone to escalation, and if they start to escalate, they are able to stop the negative process before it erupts into a full-blown, nasty fight.

Invalidation is a pattern in which one partner subtly or directly discounts or ignores the thoughts, feelings, or character of the other. Invalidation can take many forms. A most subtle form of invalidation occurs when one partner ignores the other and avoids praising them for some positive actions on their part, in order to highlight some other minor problem.

Withdrawal and avoidance are different manifestations of a pattern in which one partner shows an unwillingness to get into or stay with important discussions. Withdrawal can be as obvious as getting up and leaving the room or as subtle as "turning off" or "shutting down" during an argument. The withdrawer often ends the conversation, with no real intention of following through. When withdrawers do not feel safe, they find it difficult to identify and articulate their feelings and are particularly vulnerable to depression.

Negative interpretations occur when one partner consistently questions the motives and intentions of the other and believes them to be more negative than they really are. Such an attitude can create a very destructive, negative pattern in a relationship that makes any conflict or disagreement harder to deal with constructively. When relationships become more distressed, suspicion, doubt, and negative interpretations create an environment of hopelessness and demoralization. Negative interpretations can become very destructive, because they are very hard to detect and counteract, especially after they become cemented into the fabric of a relationship.

This discussion about the destructive forces that sabotage the marriage relationship highlights the way in which conflict, when not properly handled, is responsible for the breakdown and failure of many marriages. Couples who resort to using escalation, invalidation, or withdrawal/avoidance as a way of controlling conflict not only undermine confidence and safety within the marriage but create an atmosphere that leads to distancing and despair. When negative patterns are not confronted, challenged, or changed, real intimacy and a sense of emotional connection dies out, and couples settle for frustrated loneliness and isolation.[29]

Creative Suggestions for Managing Conflict

One of the most powerful things a couple can do to reduce distress and prevent the breakdown of their marriage is to restrain or eliminate the cycle of negativity that occurs within their relationship. They need to learn how to stop threatening, blaming, and shaming each other or using judgmental language as a way of reacting to and controlling their partner's behavior and actions. They need to learn how to manage effectively their conflict and resolve their problems in ways that protect their relationship from negativity and from those destructive interactional patterns that undermine feelings of physical safety and emotional security.

Sadly, nobody formally teaches us how to deal with conflict or negativity, so we stumble along with the attitudes and behaviors we have learned in childhood, from observing the way our parents or other significant role models dealt with their conflicts and disagreements. What we all need to embrace is a simple, easy-to-understand model of how to manage our conflict situations, so that we can stop ourselves from getting caught up in the annoying, abusive, or aggressive cycles of negativity. Outlined next is a three-step model that will help married partners connect with each other emotionally, establish a healthy dialogue, and resolve their problems amicably.

STEP ONE: CONNECT WITH THE EMOTION. In seeking to reconcile the differences between two people, the first goal in the management of marital conflict is to deal with the emotional tensions generated by the conflict and connect with the feelings of the other person. Couples need to develop a constructive process for handling the emotional components of conflict before they proceed to discuss and resolve the specific problem issue. To achieve this, they will need to focus primarily on two areas—an acknowledgement of their own feelings and responses, and a willingness to connect with the emotional reactions of their partner.

a. Calm yourself. Because being "emotionally flooded" is so destructive to a relationship, the first strategy you need to learn is to recognize when you are feeling overwhelmed, identify what triggers you, and acknowledge how you get drawn into negative patterns of interaction. Then you will need to take deliberate steps to calm yourself. Calming may involve telling yourself to become calm and relax as you monitor your physical responses, reduce your arousal level, and deal with your stress reactions, so that you can enter into dialogue with your partner. It may result in a need for you to call "time out," so you can recover your composure. Calming yourself is also achieved by talking to yourself, so that you get rid of negative, hurtful, or vengeful thoughts and replace them with soothing and validating ones that you rehearse to yourself. This will enable you to become more calm, relaxed, open, and receptive to your partner and the issue of concern.[30]

b. Listen to your partner nondefensively. Connecting with how your partner feels is crucial to understanding and resolving conflict. It helps you diffuse emotional flooding, and it will reduce the likelihood that your partner will respond defensively to you. Listening empathically enables you to embrace your partner's feelings and prevents escalation, invalidation, and withdrawal from occurring. It also helps you not to sit there analyzing your partner's motives and intentions instead of hearing what they are saying and feeling. Training yourself to speak to your partner in a way that does not trigger a negative response will reduce their defensiveness and improve your communication with each other.[31]

c. Validate each other's feelings. Accepting, appreciating, and affirming your partner's feelings does not mean you necessarily agree with them. This is not the point. Validating their experience and seeing things through their eyes shows that you empathize and understand. Nothing makes a person feel more valued, respected, and loved.[32]

STEP TWO: DISCUSS THE PROBLEM. The second goal in reconciling differences in marriage is to understand your partner's concern about a specific issue. The goal must be to seek first an understanding of their point of view before you respond and explain your position. At this stage there are a few attitudes and actions that are critical in the process of discussing the problem.

a. Make a "soft" start to the discussion. Gottman's research shows that couples in a happy, stable marriage are extremely careful about the way they begin their conflict discussions. He suggests that couples who decide on the course of "softened start-ups"[34] do so in order to minimize their partner's defensiveness. To assist in this process, they need to pay close attention to their own inner dialogue. They need to work at managing their negative thoughts and the desire to respond defensively and focus on raising issues only with friendship, sympathy, and an understanding of their partner's situation in their mind.

b. Clearly define what the problem is that needs to be resolved. Be specific, and make sure that you both understand what the nature of the problem is and how you both see the issue. Focus on one issue at a time. Do not complicate the issue by trying to discuss several different or related issues at the same time.

c. Discuss and validate your points of view. State the problem, but do not try to solve it yet. Be sure you both understand and validate each other's point of view. Do not generalize about the problem—be specific, and avoid using absolutes such as "you always," or, "you never." Avoid personally labeling each other, and seek to eliminate all hidden agendas and the use of camouflaged messages.

If discussing the problem with each other is really difficult or explosive, one or both of you may call "time out." This is not to avoid the issue but to allow time for you to calm down (return to Step One) and refocus on the substantive issues involved in the conflict. When you are ready to recommence discussions, you might wish, with respect and safety, to utilize the very effective and proven method of communicating with each other called the "speaker/listener technique," developed by Markman, Stanley, and Blumberg in their book, *Fighting for Your Marriage*.[34] This technique can operate as a "circuit breaker," by preventing the four destructive patterns of communication from emerging. It operates according to the following rules:

Rules for Couples: (a) The one speaking "has the floor" and therefore the right to speak without interruption; (b) the "floor" is shared over the course of the discussion as the couple switch roles; and (c) no problem-solving is allowed—just a good discussion of your thoughts and feelings.

Rules for the Speaker: (a) Speak for yourself. Don't try to be a mind reader. Talk about your thoughts, feelings, and concerns. Try to use "I" statements; (b) don't go on and on—confine what you say to brief, manageable statements. No long monologues; and (c) stop to let the listener paraphrase.

Rules for the Listener: (a) Paraphrase and playback what you heard; (b) focus on the speaker's message—affirm what they said. Don't try to rebut their argument.

STEP THREE: SOLVE PROBLEMS. Nothing will be resolved unless you feel positive toward one another and are invested in each other's good. Having listened to and thoroughly understood each other's point of view, you must be willing to give and take, be responsive to each other's influence, and recognize that neither of you can have your own way all the time. Furthermore, you must be prepared to cooperate mutually in bringing about changes where these are important to the relationship. Such a collaborative problem-solving process involves:[35]

a. Looking at alternative solutions. Once the problem has been adequately defined, you need to look at all the options and alternatives open to you to resolve the problem. One very useful method of achieving this is called *brainstorming*—the process of listing as many ideas as possible without criticism or evaluation.

b. Choose the best solution. After listing all your options, you now need to explore the consequences of each of the proposed alternatives. You will also need to decide which is the best solution that will have the best chance of working. To achieve this result, you will need flexibility in choosing a solution that ensures that both of your needs are met. There are at least four ways for resolving the conflict: (i) *capitulation*—you give your partner what they want; (ii) *compromise*—you both accept a final solution that goes part way toward accepting each other's view; (iii) *coexistence*—you agree to accept your current differences; and (iv) *creative solution*—where the solution is quite different from your original demands, yet satisfying to both of you.

c. Plan. Having chosen a solution, you will now need to work out an action plan and decide who will be responsible for doing what, where, and when.

d. Implement the plan. Up until this point in the process, you have done a lot of thinking and talking. Now it is time to act. By mutual agreement, the plan to resolve the problem is put into operation.

e. Evaluate the outcome and the process. Finally, you need to monitor the effect of your decision. In particular, you should check out how you felt about the process you followed, what bothers you or what you wish you had done differently, and how effective the outcome was in resolving the problem. You may even wish to set a time frame to check and see if the solution is working adequately or whether the issue needs to be revisited.

The value of this simple three-step problem-solving process is that it communicates an important, mutually affirming message to each partner about how much they each value the relationship. It conveys that they consider their partner's needs to be important enough for them to listen to and understand. It shows that they are flexible, creative, and willing to risk new pathways in their search for ideas that will improve their marriage. And it affirms their ability to share together in joint decision making that enhances their relationship and deepens their sense of loyalty and commitment and trust.

Common Mistakes in Conflict Resolution

Robert Bolton quite rightly warns us that there are a number of common mistakes made in resolving conflict effectively.[36] The first is a *failure to listen to and deal with the feelings and emotions*. When feelings are strong, they must be addressed before anything else is done.

The second mistake is a *failure to clearly define the problem*. Many people do not listen long enough to understand what the other person is saying and clearly understand their concerns.

A third mistake in conflict resolution relates to people who are in such a hurry to get to the solution stage that they **fail to get all the information** they need to understand adequately and define the problem. Until they have all the facts, they are not ready to look for a solution. Other people simply lack the desire or motivation to resolve their differences—either because they don't care anymore about the relationship, or they find it all too hard. They would sooner win by being submissive or avoiding the conflict altogether.

Finally, *failure to communicate effectively* can also create a huge barrier to conflict resolution. People who make the mistake of being critical, dogmatic, or defensive and use a range of "power plays" to block the successful resolution of conflict actively prevent their partner from feeling understood and appreciated within the marriage relationship.

Styles of Managing Conflict

Most married couples have different styles of resolving conflict when it arises within their relationship. A very practical way for them to identify and put into operation their own dominant style of conflict management is for them to explore the five major styles outlined by Kilmann and Thomas in their "Conflict Mode Instrument." This instrument (Figure 7, below) assesses the individual's behavior in conflict situations along two basic dimensions:

Assertiveness—the extent to which an individual attempts to satisfy his or her own concerns.

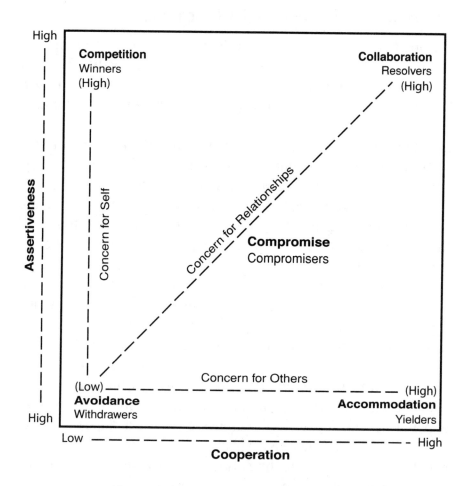

Figure 7: Styles of Conflict Management

From Jack O. Balswick and Judith K. Balswick, *The Family* (Michigan: Baker Book House, 1989), p. 220—adapted from the Kilmann-Thomas Interpersonal Conflict Mode Istrument

Cooperation—the extent to which an individual attempts to satisfy the other person's needs and concerns.

These two basic dimensions can be used to describe five spe-

	Strengths	Weaknesses
Competitive	• Measurable results • Things get done • Issues are clear • Persuasive arguments • Gets things going • Uses energy well	• Motives are misunderstood • Don't listen • Drive over people • Lonely—lacks relationships • Success driven • Guilt
Accommodator	• Seen as servant • Giving • Sacrificial • Willingness to defer	• Manipulative—"Look at me, the poor servant" • Martyr complex • Passive-aggressive • Fear of rejection—need to be liked
Collaborator	• Begin with principles of what should be • Seek to understand the whole truth • Relational • Flexible • Desire truth • Peacemaker versus peace-keeper	• Idealism is not realistic • Emotional investment is tiring • Pursuer can be seen as pushy • Disappointment and discouraged unless resolved • Patience to see everyone win • Frustration
Avoider	• Temporaty relief • Time to cool down and process through an emotion • Time to deal with me first	• Avoid problems • Communication breakdown • Inability to surface anger • Sense of superiority—"I've dealt with the problem, what about you?"
Compromiser	• Open relationships • Confidence • Reconcilers • Model of respect for others' needs • Good listener	• Feel trapped and caught in this role • Seen as weak and wishy-washy • Too long to make decisions • Wanting respect over truth

Table 6: Conflict Management Style

Adapted from Jack O. Balswick and Judith K. Balswick, D.Min. class notes, Fuller Theological Seminary, California, 1998.

cific methods or styles of dealing with conflicts, which are defined as follows:[37]

1. Competition—which involves an individual who shows a high concern for his or her own interests, less concern for their relationship, and little concern for their partner's needs. This is a power-oriented mode in which an individual stands up for his/her rights, argues, defends, and uses whatever power it takes to be a winner.

2. Accommodation—the opposite of competition. It involves individuals who show a high concern for others, less concern for their relationship, and little concern for self. There is an element of self-sacrificing in this mode as one selflessly gives, obeys, and yields to their partner's point of view.

3. Collaboration. This style involves individuals who show a high concern for their relationship and a balanced concern for self and others. They are people who work to resolve issues when two people are searching to find an alternative solution that meets both their needs or concerns.

4. Avoidance—the opposite of collaboration. It involves individuals who show little concern for self, others, and the relationship. They do not immediately address the conflict but will diplomatically sidestep the issues, postpone making a response, or withdraw from a threatening situation.

5. Compromise—involves individuals who show a moderate degree of cooperation and assertiveness. Their objective is to find expedient, mutually acceptable solutions that find the middle ground between competing and accommodating. They prefer to split the difference, exchange concessions, or seek quick, middle-ground positions.

To enjoy a healthy, balanced relationship, Christian couples are encouraged to find a balance between assertiveness and a spirit of cooperation. The most effective way to deal with conflict is a collaborative style that demonstrates an equal concern for self, the other, and the relationship. However, it is wrong to suggest that one style is inherently better or more superior than another, because different situations may elicit different styles of managing the conflict situation.

It is interesting, however, to observe how each style of conflict management has both advantages and disadvantages, depending on the situation. A brief outline of the strengths and weaknesses of each style is shown in Table 6 (page 147. One of the most common patterns that occurs in marriage—which often results in gridlock—is known as the "pursuer-distancer" relationship. The more the pursuer (resolver, compromiser, or competitor) advances, the farther away in the relationship the distancer (withdrawer or yielder) moves.[38]

Marriage brings together two people in a special relationship, each with its own unique combination of styles for handling conflict. As indicated earlier, marriage partners tend to learn their mode of conflict management in their childhood years as they are growing up in their family of origin, where they observe, copy, and react to the styles of their parents. As a result, couples can sometimes find themselves gridlocked in conflict, using two learned styles that don't work well together. This can be frustrating and confusing, especially if they both believe innately that their way is right and that it is the only way to manage the conflict and achieve resolution, peace, and harmony.

Notes:

1. Howard Markman, Scott Stanley, and Susan Blumberg, *Fighting for Your Marriage* (San Francisco: Jossey-Bass Publishers, 1994), p. 6.

2. Virginia Satir, *Peoplemaking* (Palo Alto, Calif.: Science and Behaviour Books, 1972), p. 138.

3. John Gottman, *Why Marriages Succeed or Fail* (New York: Simon and Schuster, New York, 1994), p. 28.

4. Susan M. Johnson, *Creating Connection* (New York: Brunner/Mazel, 1996), pp. 1, 3.

5. Susan M. Johnson and Leslie S. Greenberg, *The Heart of the Matter* (New York: Brunner/Mazel, 1994), pp. 302, 309.

6. Susan M. Johnson and Leslie Greenberg, "The Emotionally Focused Approach to Problems in Adult Attachment," in *Clinical Handbook of Couple Therapy,* by Neil Jacobson and Alan Gurman (New York: Guilford Press, 1995), pp. 121-126.

7. Ibid.

8. John Gottman, *Why Marriages Succeed or Fail,* pp. 56-67.

9. Robert Bolton, *People Skills* (New Jersey: Prentice Hall, Inc., 1979), p. 207.

10. Jack Dominian, *Marriage* (London: Heinemann, 1995), p. 87.

11. H. Newton Malony, *When Getting Along Seems Impossible* (New Jersey: Fleming H. Revell, 1989), pp. 15, 18, 31.

12. Robert Bolton, *People Skills,* p. 217.

13. John Gottman and Nan Silver, *The Seven Principles of Making Marriage Work,* (New York: Crown Publishers, Inc., 1999), p. 135.

14. Ibid., pp. 130-132.

15. Robert J. Sternberg and Mahzad Hojjat, eds., *Satisfaction in Close Relationships* (New York: Guilford Press, 1997), pp. 259-262.

16. John Gottman, *Why Marriages Succeed or Fail,* pp. 149-153.

17. John Gottman, *The Marriage Clinic* (New York: W.W. Norton and Company, 1999), p. 307.

18. Howard Markman, Scott Stanley, and Susan Blumberg, *Fighting for Your Marriage* (San Francisco: Jossey-Bass Publishers, 1994), pp. 123-131.

19. Ibid., p. 132.

20. John Gottman, *Why Marriages Succeed or Fail,* pp. 57-61.

21. Kathleen M. Galvin and Bernard J. Brommel, *Family Communications* (Illinois: Scott Foresman and Company, 1982), p. 192.

22. Jon Carlson and Len Sperry, *The Intimate Couple* (Philadelphia: Brunner/Mazel, 1999), p. 300.

23. Everett L. Worthington, Jr., *Marriage Counseling* (Illinois: InterVarsity Press, 1989), pp. 265, 266.

24. Carlfred Broderick, *Couples* (New York: Simon and Schuster, 1979), p. 91.

25. John Gottman, *Why Marriages Succeed or Fail*, pp. 72-79.

26. Ibid., p. 97.

27. John Gottman and Nan Silver, *The Seven Principles of Making Marriage Work*, p. 72.

28. Howard Markman, Scott Stanley, and Susan Blumberg, *Fighting for Your Marriage*, pp. 14-30.

29. Ibid., p. 30.

30. John Gottman, *Why Marriages Succeed or Fail,* pp. 176-181.

31. Ibid., pp. 181-194.

32. Ibid., pp. 195-199.

33. John Gottman, The Marriage Clinic, 224, 225.

34. Howard Markman, Scott Stanley, and Susan Blumberg, *Fighting for Your Marriage,* pp. 63, 64.

35. Victor J. Callan and Patricia Noller, *Marriage and the Family* (Australia: Methuen, 1987), p. 154.

36. Robert Bolton, *People Skills,* pp. 253, 254.

37. Jack O. Balswick and Judith K. Balswick, *The Family* (Michigan: Baker Book House, 1991), pp. 220-222.

38. Jack O. Balswick and Judith K. Balswick, *The Dual-Earner Marriage* (Michigan: Fleming H. Revell, 1995), pp. 68, 69.

SIX

Common Emotional Obstacles in Marriage

The key to marital intimacy is emotional connection. The sense of connection grows out of a relationship between two married people that is based on honest communication, mutual respect, and emotional equality. This sense of equality and emotional closeness begins to emerge as the couple engages in the process of intimately sharing their thoughts, feelings, and experiences with each other in ways that are both rewarding and deeply meaningful.

However, as Karen Prager points out, intimacy also creates a dilemma. It makes individuals emotionally vulnerable to one another.[1] Two people cannot live together and love each other without getting to know their partner extremely well. This, of course, opens up the possibility that one partner may attack the other's weaknesses or exploit their vulnerabilities in ways that leave them feeling exposed, defenseless, hurt, resentful, or even abandoned. When actions such as this occur, they generate a great degree of negative emotion and become a source of distress and anxiety as the marital bond is placed under threat.

Intimacy Threatened by Stress, Anger, and Depression

How couples deal with and resolve the negative emotion in their marriage is both challenging and difficult. Intimacy in marriage can so easily be threatened by experiences of stress, conflict, and anger. Yet no one formally teaches us how to deal with these major issues, in spite of the fact that they constitute some of the most common obstacles to achieving intimacy in marriage.

Influenced by their own personality and life experiences, couples frequently use different ways of dealing with these issues, which in themselves often create more conflict and stress within the relationship. Furthermore, most partners have different capacities for tolerating stress and disagreements, and these have the potential of creating further feelings of inadequacy, misunderstanding, and disconnnection. Tired, frustrated, and hurt, they resort to withdrawing emotionally and distancing themselves from their partner and from the negative feelings created by their destructive interactions.

In this chapter, we explore the way in which levels of stress, the presence of anger, and the experience of depression impact the marriage relationship and block the pathway to intimacy. Couples need to be able to understand and define the emotional components involved in these issues and identify the causes that give rise to distress and dysfunction in relationships as a result of these issues. Finally, we will offer a range of practical suggestions and guidelines on how to deal more effectively with these three common obstacles to intimacy in marriage.

Effects of Stress on Couple Satisfaction

In today's world, stress has become a household word and a common term for identifying the causes and emotional consequences of our struggle to manage the pressures of daily living. Never has there been such a widespread interest in preventing, managing, and eliminating stress from our lives.[2] While we learn to live with stress, the pressure of conflicting responsibilities, tight schedules and deadlines, and personal commitments all take their toll. Hans Selye, the distinguished Austrian physiologist, said:

> The greatest cause of distress for humankind living in an
> environment of disharmony is the stress of living with one
> another...It isn't technology which threatens to undermine the

quality of our lives but rather the unmitigated selfishness in our relationships. Through these feelings of mutual indifference we co-exist but we certainly don't co-operate with each other.[3]

Couples will appreciate that there are a number of stressful life experiences that can have a very negative and destructive effect on their marriage, dramatically reducing the level of satisfaction they enjoy with their partner. These experiences fall into three categories:

1. Major life events or developmental issues that are so disruptive and threatening that they require individual partners to make a major adjustment to their relationship. Events such as the birth of a child, the transition to parenthood, dealing with teenagers, the loss of a job, or the death of a family member, can create tremendous stress in the marriage.

2. Environmental, economic, or living conditions that create ongoing stressful situations that constantly intrude into the relationship. Circumstances, problems, and difficulties such as unemployment, high workloads, inability to pay one's bills, living in an unsafe neighborhood, or dealing with family illness, impact the marriage in significant ways.

3. Minor stressors or frustration demands that create aggravation and annoyance and affect the individual partners' everyday lives. These stressors include such things as role overload, fighting peak-hour traffic, having too many things to do, and being overly concerned about one's weight or appearance.[4]

Research indicates that stress has a tendency to increase conflict and dissatisfaction in the marriage relationship, and where one or both of the partners have a heavy workload, there is a greater likelihood that there will be recurring negative interactional patterns between the couple. When the experience of stress is particularly disabling, partners who tend to look to each other for increased emotional support frequently find that they have a decreased ability to give support to their partner and thereby nurture the relationship. In fact, some studies have shown that partners experiencing high levels of stress tend to have a much greater self-focus and are therefore less able to understand and appreciate their partner's needs or points of view. Often when stress dominates the relationship, it tends to exacerbate old conflicts of interest and may even be responsible for generating new conflicts within the relationship.[5]

Further indications exist that when people are stressed, they tend to use defensive communication styles, which alienates their partner. Some see the four styles of communication developed by Satir (see chapter 3) as styles that express individual stress growing out of feelings of fear, anxiety, and low self-esteem.[6] Prager's research clearly shows that intimacy not only serves as a wonderful "buffer against the pathogenic effects of stress, but that it promotes individual health and well-being."[7]

In her book *Stress and the Healthy Family,* Delores Curran lists the top ten situations that married men and women identified as being stressful for them in their marriage and family life. The top stresses, in order of priority, are:

▶ Economics/finances/budgeting

▶ Children's behavior/discipline/sibling fighting

▶ Insufficient couple time

▶ Lack of shared responsibility in the family

▶ Communicating with children

▶ Insufficient "me" time

▶ Guilt for not accomplishing more

▶ Spousal relationship (communication, friendship, sex)

▶ Insufficient family playtime

▶ Overscheduled family calendar[8]

Couples under stress consistently indicate that they are dissatisfied with both their marriage and the quality of their lives.[9] When they reach the point of stress overload, they usually display the following symptoms:

▶ They feel a sense of being driven, they feel a loss of energy, and they become concerned about unrelenting feelings of fatigue.

▶ They have a desire to get away from people and pressures.

▶ They frequently demonstrate an argumentative or condemning attitude.

▶ They have a tendency to live in the past or the future.

▶ They experience a pervasive sense of guilt about not being or doing everything for the people in their life.

▶ They are often touchy and react with sharp words.

▶ They tend to view God as punitive and demanding.

▶ They have little time to listen to and connect with others.

▶ They often feel that they are a failure.

▶ They have a tendency to blame others rather than seek solutions to their problems.

Individuals who have a highly stressed partner tend to be very resentful of their workload and the fact that they have little time and energy to invest in the marriage relationship.[10]

How to Manage Marital Stress

Stress is a physiological reaction of the body to a real or perceived emergency situation. This "flight or fight" response results from the injection of several hormones into the bloodstream that prepares the body for action or defense. The major stress-related hormone is adrenaline (the energy hormone) which raises the heart rate and the cholesterol levels in the body to fight the emergency.

However, prolonged stress is very bad for the body and for relationships. The body does not handle extended periods of adrenaline stimulation. Eventually, it experiences adrenaline exhaustion, which depletes the immune system, creates fatigue, and is linked to heart attacks and excess cholesterol in the body.

In today's materialistic world, where the emphasis is on status and performance, couples need to be aware of the harmful effects of stress on their bodies and learn how to manage it so it doesn't unbalance and destroy their relationship. Here then are a few practical suggestions on how couples can manage stress more effectively.

1. Identify the source of your anxiety and stress. To start with, try to discover what people, issues, or events press your buttons and increase your stress. Knowing what your top stressors are can help you avoid and reduce your levels of stress. It is also important to slow down and recognize your limits and the "tolerance level" of your partner as well. Recognizing what creates anxiety and tension is a vital first step to managing your stress.

2. Prioritize your activities. Take time to organize yourself and establish realistic goals for the accomplishment of those things most important to your health and happiness. Stop trying to accomplish so many things. It is time to edit your life and your possessions, drop any nonproductive activities, and weed out those things that clutter your life and waste time. The purpose of this exercise is to set priorities and maintain a balanced lifestyle that keeps the important things in perspective. Vital resources to reducing stress are daily activities such as good nutrition, adequate sleep, and regular exercise. Once you have established your priorities, stay with them. Don't obligate yourself to take on things that do not fit with your priorities.

3. Set boundaries. One of the hardest things for highly motivated people to do is to say "No." Learning to clearly set your own personal boundaries protects you and helps you prevent others from placing demands on you that imbalance your life. Balancing work, church, and family responsibilities requires the ability to say No to things that rob you of valuable time to relax and enjoy your marriage and family relationships. Dealing with over-commitment is one of the greatest stressors in family life.

4. Communicate more with each other. It is a fact that when stress increases, communication decreases, and couples stop listening and talking to each other. Deal with your differences, and stop blaming others and responding with a negative attitude and tone of voice. These types of responses only increase stress. Couples who share their thoughts, feelings, and concerns with each other tend to generate more positive feedback and solutions to the things that concern them.

5. Enforce a time for recovery. The fundamental issue in stress management is learning how to manage your bodily reactions to adrenaline. Many individuals are quite vulnerable to stress and to the effects of adrenaline, because these effects often leave them feeling good. So knowing and anticipating those times when you are depleted requires awareness and vigilance. In order for your personal resources to be renewed, you need to enforce an adequate time for recovery that allows for relaxation, sleep, and exercise. These are essential for managing stress—especially sleep, which is the primary way we recover from adrenaline exhaustion.

6. Regularly spend time together. Spending time together to build a healthy, stable relationship with your partner is one of the best ways to reduce and manage stress. Time spent playing, laughing, and relaxing renews your momentum, increases alertness and concentration, and helps you get things done. The emotional energy that is generated from closeness and connection with your partner enables you to keep things in perspective and realize the importance that relationships play in our physical health and emotional well being.

7. Maintain a support network. Couples who develop a network of people who understand and support them emotionally tend to be less self-focused, intense, and stressed-out about life. The feeling that you belong to a healthy, robust community of friends that you enjoy and desire to be with is therapeutic and builds in both of you a sense of self-confidence, esteem, and belonging.

Anger in Marriage

The expression and experience of anger is another very significant obstacle married partners have to deal with in marriage. It is, in fact, the most common emotion demonstrated by couples[11] and constitutes the supreme manifestation of the struggle for power and control in all close relationships. When individuals get angry, they become energized by a power that can fill their mind and take possession of their whole being. Many do not realize just how much their anger can influence their behavior and color their perceptions of themselves, others, or their world. They fail to recognize just how quickly anger can damage their marriage relationship and destroy their love for one another.

Anger is often a much greater problem in marriage than it is in any other relationship, because couples are living in close contact and interacting with each other every day. They can so easily get upset and angry with one another as they wrestle with their differences—or become annoyed and frustrated when their partner will not change or submit to their influence and control. Furthermore, their marriage relationship can become extremely vulnerable to tension and stress when they offload or dump on each other the angry feelings that really belong to other people, situations, or extended family members.[12]

The impact experienced by marriages that end up absorbing a lot of anger and negativity can be quite devastating. Couples who do not properly understand or process their anger run the risk that the warmth, closeness, and intimacy they crave in their relationship will be frustrated and denied. When two people engage each other in repeated episodes of angry exchanges, they rapidly build barriers of fear and distrust that only make them become more rigid and highly defensive toward each other in their relationship. By using methods that are clearly counter-productive, they increase feelings of disconnection and generate a sense of alienation and hopelessness.

Some people, unfortunately, live with the illusion that a good marriage must be an anger-free relationship. They believe that the sign of a happy, healthy marriage is that a couple are so committed to each other that they never argue, disagree, or get angry with one another. Such a delusion can only be achieved by two people who have a total commitment to "peace at all costs" and who hide natural feelings and emotions beneath a veneer of niceness, pretense, and avoidance, unaware of their denial or their distortion of reality.[13]

Confusion About Anger

A great deal of confusion exists about anger and the role it plays in relationships. Some see it as a powerful but healthy emotion—a *feeling* that must be contained or it will easily escalate out of control and become negative and destructive. Some classify anger as an explosive, hostile, and aggressive **behavior** that seeks to dominate, manipulate, and control other people. Others see it as a *cognitive* process that interprets the motives and actions of another person and consciously selects concrete ways of thinking and responding to them that are manifest in attitudes of irritation, hatred, self-pity, emotional restraint, low self-esteem, pessimism, and verbal or physical aggression.[14]

Since anger involves all three of these components—emotional, cognitive, and behavioral—we cannot limit our definition and understanding of it to just the behavioral or observable dimension. It is a complex response that exists inside people, and we need to make a careful distinction between feelings of anger and the choices people make to express their anger through their behavior.[15] Anger is a normal, natural, God-given "emotional response that involves a specific set of thoughts, bodily reactions, facial expressions and behavioural actions."[16] Because this definition includes the cognitive process, it follows that anger need not be seen as an evil, uncontrollable emotion but as one which can be managed and controlled in constructive ways.[17]

Anger and the Bible

Christian couples are frequently caught in a struggle over anger that leaves them feeling confused and bewildered. Down through the centuries, the church fathers have consistently presented anger as evil—a sinful behavior, a sign of the devil's presence on earth. As a result, the church has tended to focus mostly on the behavioral aspects of anger and ignore the existence of anger as a legitimate feeling or emotion. Consequently, it highlights those scriptures that reflect the sinfulness of anger and its association with the "old nature."

"Get rid of all bitterness, rage and anger" (Ephesians 4:31; Colossians 3:8, NIV).

"An angry man stirs up dissension and a hot-tempered one commits many sins," (Proverbs 29:22, NIV).

Don't even "associate with one easily angered, or you may learn his ways" (Proverbs 22:24, 25, NIV).

"Anyone who is angry with his brother will be subject to judgment" (Matthew 5:22, NIV).

This emphasis clearly reflects the dangers associated with anger that is poorly managed, but overlooks the fact that scripture also sees anger as a normal human emotion.

The Old Testament clearly recognizes God's experience of anger by declaring that He is "compassionate and gracious, slow to anger" and someone who will "not harbour his anger forever" (Psalm 103:8, 9, NIV). There is never any suggestion that God's anger is sinful, nor is there any biblical support for the idea that Jesus' anger was evil or sinful either (Mark 3:1-5; John 2:13-15). When speaking about anger, the New Testament writers use several different Greek words to describe a wide range of feelings associated with anger. The various degrees of intensity experienced when one is angry are reflected in words that incorporate the inner attitudes of irritation, indignation, bitterness and resentment, and the demonstrable behaviors of aggressiveness, hostility, and outrage.

The apostle Paul clearly makes the distinction between anger as a feeling and anger as a chosen behavior, in his counsel to the believers at Ephesus, when he says:

> Go ahead and be angry. You do well to be angry—but do not use your anger as fuel for revenge. And don't stay angry. Don't go to bed angry. Don't give the Devil that kind of foothold in your life. (Ephesians 4:26, *THE MESSAGE.*)

Here Paul does not condemn the emotion of anger as sin. He accepts it as a normal part of human experience—an experience we do well to recognize and affirm.

However, he is also quick to point out that the way we deal with our angry feelings can easily lead us to choose destructive behaviors capable of seriously affecting our relationship with others and encouraging evil to take possession of our heart and life. He goes on, therefore, to command that we do everything by God's grace and power to manage our anger, by avoiding those choices that lead us to hold on to bitterness and resentment, seek revenge, or explode with hostility and rage. (Ephesians 4:31.)

Clearly, anger must be seen as a gift—a natural endowment which is part of the human condition.[18] It is a natural response to the stress, frustration, and disagreements that occur in marriage; it constitutes our own innate way of defending ourselves. As Gottman asserts, anger is not a dangerous or destructive emotion,[19] it only has a negative effect in marriage if it is expressed along with criticism, contempt, or defensiveness,[20] or if an individual refuses to explore, communicate, and deal with it openly and honestly with their partner.[21]

A Model for Understanding Anger

A proper understanding of anger and how it works is absolutely essential if couples are to build a stable, healthy marriage relationship. A failure on their part to acknowledge the powerful role anger plays in their marriage can be extremely distressing to them and hazardous to their health and emotional well-being. Many may know from experience what anger feels like, but do they know how it works?

Anger has been defined as "a strong feeling of displeasure, excited by a real or supposed injury; often accompanied by a desire to take revenge or to obtain satisfaction from the offending party."[23] This definition suggests that there are three components to anger and that these concepts help us understand what anger is and how it works:

1. An injury. We are frustrated, threatened, or hurt by someone or something that appears to—or actually does—personally attack our goals, plans, or self-esteem.

2. A strong feeling. Anger is a secondary emotion that comes to warn us that we have been personally attacked.

3. A desire for revenge or resolution. We make a choice about how we will manage our feelings and emotional reactions.

When couples experience feelings of anger in their marriage, the anger operates as a possible survival emotion that has two very distinct purposes:

It acts as a warning to let them know that they have been hurt, that their personal or relational goals have been ignored or frustrated, or that their boundaries have been violated or some injustice has occurred. In this sense, it protects them from further harm and helps them to defend their personal dignity, respect, and worth from further attack.

It acts as a motivator, energizing them to overcome whatever physical or emotional obstacles they may be facing, not by dominating or causing injury to their partner, but by enabling them to gather and use those resources than can produce healing, reconciliation, and growth in the relationship. This implies that besides alleviating and overcoming their own frustrations, their anger also motivates them to address the anger of their partner and provide the means for them to regain their respect and independence. In this way, it changes anger from being a one-sided game entailing compliance, to an active, two-sided argument in which two people seek to influence each other and redefine their boundaries.[22]

Dr. Arch Hart proposes a simple linear model (see Figure 8, facing page) that outlines in general terms the essential elements involved in understanding the nature of anger and how it is typically resolved. This model consists of four levels and features the origins and causes of anger, two modes of anger expression, and four common methods used in the resolution of anger.[24] It also provides the structure for further exploration of the biblical concept of forgiveness and how couples can learn to overcome their personal hurt and pain and let go of their bitterness and the desire for revenge in their relationship with one another.

The Origins of Anger. Hart suggests that our anger response is both biological (instinctual) and learned. In the first instance, it is one of the primary emotions we are all born with that protects us and enables our survival. But most of our anger is triggered by the way we interpret certain events that confront us in our environment. Once our cognitive processes have triggered our anger, it also becomes a biological state as well.

The Causes of Anger. Any incident, regardless of how trivial

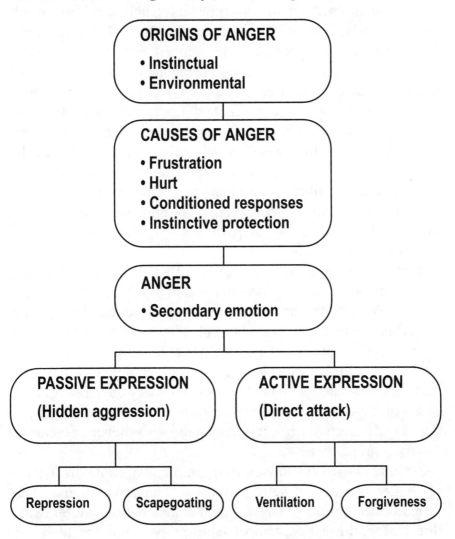

Figure 8: A Model for Understanding Anger

Adapted from Archibald D. Hart, *Unlocking the Mystery of Your Emotions* (Dallas: Word Publishing, 1989), p. 47.

it is, can serve as a trigger to release stored-up anxiety, frustration, or resentment. When anger explodes, couples are often surprised and bewildered by the strength of the feeling that is released. The four main causes of anger are:

1. Frustration. Anything that prevents an individual from reaching their goals or getting what they need or desire has the potential for creating anger. These obstacles may either be physical (a broken lawn mower), social (we lose someone or something important to us; someone refuses to respect us), or personal (feelings of inadequacy or low self-esteem). And it may include conflict situations in which an individual is torn between two or more competing goals. The fifteen different behaviors Buss identified that can evoke anger in marriage include being moody, abusive, condescending, unfaithful, inconsiderate, disheveled, emotionally constricted, sexually aggressive/withholding, possessive, jealous, self-centered, insulting your partner's appearance, or being neglectful and unreliable [25]

2. Hurt. Another important cause of anger is hurt, which can arise whenever we experience physical or psychological pain. The pain we experience when someone demeans, belittles, humiliates, criticizes or uses sarcasm to abuse or ridicule us can not only trigger an angry response but a strong desire to defend ourselves and retaliate by hurting the other person back as much as they have hurt us. Over-reaction to being hurt is probably the most common cause of anger in relationships, especially marriage, and is particularly destructive when it is associated with silence or contempt toward your partner.

3. Conditioned responses. Early in life, we learn how to show our anger as a way of getting what we want from others. These "conditioned" forms of anger may include pouting, withdrawing, threatening, throwing a temper tantrum, becoming negative, being uncooperative or abusive, or using emotional blackmail as a way of manipulating others to give in and respond to our demands. We quickly learn that these behaviors work for us when they are reinforced and rewarded by others giving in and giving us what we want.

4. Instinctive protection. When faced with life-threatening obstacles, and our survival is at risk, anger can provide the energy and motivation to fight off the threat. This healthy form of anger is not often required in today's world where the threat to our daily security is low.

When individuals respond emotionally to any one of these causes, we need to recognize that the anger that results is a secondary emotion. In other words, it is the emotion that follows prior events and feelings. The anger has been triggered by another emotion which is deeper down, and it is only when we get back to the underlying primary emotion and deal with it, that the particular source of our anger can be located, clarified, and removed.[26]

One of the cardinal rules for helping couples resolve their anger is to encourage them to first acknowledge the presence of anger and then connect with the frustration, hurt, and pain behind the anger. Their anger is merely the signal that deeper down, there lies the source of their pain. By recognizing the anger and exploring the reasons for the hurt and pain, couples find the pathway that leads to understanding, resolution, and connection.

The modes of anger expression. People tend to develop either positive or negative ways of expressing their anger. Negative styles tend to focus more on individuals who are driven by their angry feelings to such an extent that they either over control (passively hiding their aggression) or under control (actively express their rage) them. Couples who deal with their anger in destructive ways end up attacking and wounding each other. The result is usually hurt, hate, and severe harm to their relationship. Unfortunately, too many couples come to accept this style of expressing their anger as normal and acceptable, without realizing that it is ripping apart the very foundation of their love. Their anger ceases to be a signal that something is wrong and that someone is hurting.

Positive styles focus on individuals who actively acknowledge and control their angry feelings so that they remain free to act purposefully and constructively in resolving their differences and misunderstandings. Dealing with anger constructively enables couples to express their negative feelings without attacking each other. As they communicate, inform, and connect with each other, they not only survive their anger but they benefit from the experience as it opens up opportunities for greater intimacy and closeness.[27]

Methods of resolving anger. Hart proposes four different methods that are typically used to resolve anger. Three of these methods—repression, scapegoating, and ventilation—are quite inadequate for dealing with anger and building a strong marriage relationship. The fourth method—the process of forgiveness—undoubtedly offers the most positive, constructive, and fruitful approach to the problem of anger.

1. Repression of anger. Putting anger down and forcing it out of your awareness has always been known to be harmful to mental health and ultimately destructive to relationships. Repression of anger acts like a toxin, poisoning the spirit and damaging the body. It usually creates psychosomatic complaints, muscular fatigue, and gastric disturbances. It can also distort a person's perspective on life, causing them to become cynical and miserable. When an individual does seek to hide their feelings by "stuffing them inside," clamming up, or retreating into silence, they run the risk of nursing their bitterness and resentment, denying reality, and becoming depressed.

2. Scapegoating. This method is very common in relationships and refers to the tendency to take the anger that belongs in one place and dump it on another so that you can escape the consequences of the problem. One of the first things people in conflict tend to do is take their anger out on someone else or look for someone to blame. By blaming, the angry person feels they have the right to hold the other person accountable for their own actions.

3. Ventilation. Those who advocate catharsis assert that venting feelings of anger and hostility is the best way to release anger and resolve problems—that expressing your anger at a person, especially the one who deserves it, will clear the air and ease the spirit. However, as Carol Tavris and others have pointed out, exploding with rage does not necessarily make things better. "Expressing anger while you feel angry nearly always makes you angrier. . . . Venting anger," she says, "is not much different from staying silent if our expressions of anger serve to block change rather than facilitate it."[28] So, while expressing anger in an open, aggressive way may feel very satisfying to an angry person, overwhelming another with rage and hostility only tends to court abuse. Even between equals, a display of anger can cause more trouble than it dispels, and it may simply lead a couple to fight rather than negotiate.[29]

4. Forgiveness. The act of forgiveness offers the best solution to the resolution of anger. After all, anger is a sign of attachment[30]— evidence that we care about someone enough to respond to the frustrations, threats, and hurts they create in us. So knowing how to connect with them, say we're sorry, or surrender the right to hurt them back offers the most effective way to deal with our anger. God calls us to be forgivers, not attackers.

How to Manage Anger in Marriage

The sixteenth-century essayist Montaigne once wrote that "there is no passion like anger to shake the clarity of our judgment."[31] It is so powerful it is capable of blocking our ability to love one another and hide our acute hurts and emotional pains. It is not something to be repressed or celebrated but something that requires very careful attention, monitoring, and management.

The apostle Paul encourages us to "keep a sharp eye out for the weeds of bitter discontent" and commands us to deal promptly with our anger when it occurs. "Don't stay angry. Don't use your anger as fuel for revenge." He further instructs us not to "hit back" or "insist on getting even" but rather to discover the beauty in everyone and "surprise them with goodness" (Hebrews 12:15; Ephesians 4:26; Romans 12:17, 19, *THE MESSAGE*). Clearly, he sees anger as a tool for living—an instrument capable of producing great harm or wonderful harmony.

Giving expression to your anger is healthy for your marriage and likely to promote greater relationship satisfaction. Here, then, are a few positive suggestions on how to carefully manage your anger more effectively so that it does not get out of control and become destructive.

1. Recognize and admit that you are angry. Because most of us try to avoid and deny anger in our relationships, we often find it hard to recognize its presence, especially before it escalates and explodes out of control. Acknowledging anger in yourself or your partner requires empathy, honesty, and a willingness to communicate openly with each other about how you are feeling. But hiding your anger and pretending it does not exist only complicates matters and makes resolution more difficult.

2. Watch your attitude. When you feel under attack, the natural reaction is to become defensive. A defensive attitude makes you focus more on your own integrity and survival and less on the need to connect, understand, and be responsive to your partner's concern and feelings. It also generates a strong urge to launch a blistering counterattack to get revenge. This vindictive attitude can become a barrier in two ways: (a) it shows a lack of respect for your partner's concerns and feelings, and (b) it tends to destroy the feeling of emotional safety in the relationship, creating defensiveness on both sides.

3. Concentrate on connecting, not winning. Because anger has the ability to create defensiveness, try to speak calmly and slowly, talking to each other in terms of hurt feelings, not personal faults. Don't start blaming or attacking each other's vulnerabilities, but seek to understand your partner's point of view. Allow them to explain how they feel, while you listen and try to connect with the frustration and hurt. Don't sit there making interpretations about their motives or intentions, but seek to paraphrase what you hear and provide feedback that lets them know that you connect and understand.

4. Stay focused. Do not be bothered by every little thing that is said. Recognize that when anger is aroused, we all have the ability to exaggerate, make threats, or overstate the case. Be focused. Hear the intensity of the concern. Try to identify the basic cause of your partner's anger, accurately diagnose what provoked it, and stay focused on that issue or topic. Learn to respond only to the important issue, and keep quiet about the trivial things. Anger is more easily managed when you restrain (not deny or repress) your emotional response, control the emotional aspects of the discussion, try not to escalate the feelings, exaggerate your concerns, or make threats (such as leaving or ending the relationship).

5. Acknowledge your part in the problem. As you explore the issue and connect with each other's feelings, be willing to take responsibility for the part you have played in the problem. It really is important that as you share your complaints and criticisms, you also affirm each other and each other's perspective and take ownership of those things you have done to cause offense, injury, or misunderstanding.

6. Be willing to say you're sorry. Be prepared to forgive each other for hurts caused and wrongs committed and "make up." Saying you are sorry does not mean you necessarily take all the responsibility (especially if wrongs have occurred on both sides), but "I'm sorry" does need to be said promptly, sincerely, and unconditionally. Making excuses, delaying, or withdrawing without giving assurances that the issue is understood and resolved, can be used as a further way of punishing your partner and keeping the issue alive.

7. Repair hurt feelings. Once the fight is over, it is time to replenish the relationship and repair the hurt feelings that remain. There are three basic ways to approach the healing process: (a) *apologize*—for anything that was unfair, exaggerated, or spoken in the heat of the moment which may have offended or wounded your partner; (b) *assure*—your partner that you love, respect, and support them and value the relationship, even if you both feel differently about a specific issue; and (c) *accept*—that your partner's ideas, feelings, and explanations may be different than yours, but that this is alright. No one needs to be a total winner or loser. Accept that there may be more time needed for a fuller understanding to emerge.[32]

What to Do Before and After Anger Strikes

The best possible time to develop effective strategies in your anger management plan is when you are calm and relaxed. By carefully examining your attitudes and behaviors, you can learn how to make changes and discipline yourself to respond more appropriately to outbursts of anger when they occur in the marriage. There are three important challenges that need to be considered:

1. Identify your anger style. The first challenge is to diagnose accurately your own style of expressing anger and understand what sort of issues typically trigger it. Are you in touch with your feelings? What do you do with your hurt? What is your tolerance level for dealing with frustration? How do you come across to your partner? Are you impatient, aggressive, or demanding? What message does your tone of voice convey? How competitive are you, and how do you respond to someone who thwarts your efforts or puts you down? Are you a good loser? Do you handle change graciously? Are you rigid, unforgiving, and always invested in being right? Answering these kinds of questions about your own ways of handling anger will help you establish a more realistic appraisal of your relational style and enable you to affirm those changes needed to improve your methods of resolving anger.

2. Deal with resentment and rage. You need to recognize that when you choose to hide your hurts and repress your anger, you run the risk that they will quickly turn into bitterness, resentment, and rage, leaving you feeling the victim of your partner's harsh and unjust treatment. Typically, when a problem is not resolved, and you keep ruminating about it, you begin to feel resentful toward your partner. The more you dwell on the issue, the more your injuries feel unforgivable. When your attitude becomes more settled, you begin to develop a deep-seated feeling of hatred and resentment.

Broderick suggests that "there is no human trait that is more destructive than the hoarding of resentment."[33] He describes six common ways that couples deal with these deep-seated resentments. Typically, these "power struggles" are characterized by ambivalent, stubborn, nagging, domineering, apathetic, or passive-aggressive behaviors. Their resentment eventually takes over the marriage, and they find it hard to enjoy anything. It leaves them feeling so full of anger that they can hardly think of anything else. They feel irritated with each other and frequently do and say things they later regret.

When an individual gives up all thought of resolving their frustrations, their anger becomes so intense that it turns into rage. Rage is always self-defeating because it loses sight of the reason for its existence and strives only to hurt and injure the other person. Clouded by passion and a chance to get even, enraged individuals can destroy all that they love, including themselves. Dealing with and resolving feelings of rage and resentment are a vital way of preventing anger from getting out of control and dominating the relationship.

3. Learn to be forgiving. Forgiveness is the antidote to anger—the most crucial step in neutralizing anger's destructive power in a marriage relationship. That is why married couples need to understand what it is, learn what it involves, and practice it in their relationship. Forgiveness is a voluntary choice—an attitude that leads to healing and reconciliation. It is not a feeling but a behavioral process that involves:

a. Accepting the hurt and anger—not denying or pretending it does not exist or that it is not real.

b. Claiming the right to seek justice from the other person for violating you.

c. Choosing to give up the right to retaliate and demand that the one violating you make things right.

d. Accepting that forgiveness is an act of grace—an unnatural human act that grows out of a desire to let go of the past. This does not mean forgetting what has happened but detaching from the pain that links the soul to injury.

e. Seeking to confront the offender (which is not always possible), in order to be redemptive and experience healing and a new sense of well-being in relationship. This action seeks to re-open the future and reach out in mutual forgiveness and acceptance to reestablish community.

Augsburger asserts that authentic forgiveness . . .

> is marked by a reconciliation in which there is movement by both partners toward each other, cessation of continuing animosity over the injury and a re-opening of the future in trust as each accepts both the good and bad parts of the self and the other.[34]

The ultimate goal of forgiveness is to heal old wounds so that community is restored and we can get on with our lives and enjoy greater intimacy and satisfaction in our marriage.

Depression in Marriage

A good, healthy, stable marriage relationship involves two people with a deeply committed love for each other who mutually enjoy a sense of intimacy, closeness, and optimism, effective communication, and sexual satisfaction. The feelings that they have about themselves and their marriage are determined to a large extent by how well they get along with each other and how well their marriage lives up to expectations. If, however, the marriage becomes difficult or stressful because their needs and expectations are not met, and there are strong feelings of detachment and hostility, the relationship may become a trigger for depression in one or both of the partners.

Depression is one of the most common psychiatric illnesses in our world today, and it impinges heavily on the marriage relationship. Individuals who suffer from depression are more likely to have problems in their marriage, with the result that the marriage itself becomes depressed.[35] Research makes it clear that when partners lose their ability to have fun together, enjoy each other's company, and instead focus only on the negatives, the likelihood of depression increases. According to Michael Yapko, at least 50 percent of people diagnosed as depressed are having marital problems, and at least 50 percent of those who seek therapy for marital problems are depressed. The evidence, he says, is that . . .

Marital distress often precedes depression, martial conflict is highly predictive of later depression, and an increase in marital conflict related to other stressful life events is a most common trigger for depression.[36]

Factors That Lead to Depression in Marriage

Depression in marriage results from a sense of our helplessness and hopelessness about restoring a worthwhile life following feelings of loss. While being emotional, depression is not a single emotion but a complex emotional state that consists of a mixture of anxiety, anger, guilt, and shame. These are the emotions of struggle that fight against accepting the finality of the loss. The anxiety is about loss of identity, the anger is about resentment that nothing was done to save the situation, the guilt results from feeling that we may be responsible for the failure and loss, and the shame arises from the sense that the loss reflects badly on our character.

Research indicates that a wide range of factors lead to depression in marriage. Married partners greatly benefit from recognizing the way in which the following factors can trigger depression in one of both of them, or their relationship:[37]

1. The quality of the marriage. If couples feel a sense of failure or disappointment about the way they connect with each other, how they interact and communicate together, and how they reconcile their differences, this can be a powerful factor in creating depression in marriage.

2. Marital discord and negativity. Depression often results when couples feel worn down by constant fighting and the critical attacks of their partner. Furthermore, when partners feel negative or depressed, the interpretation they place on their partner's behavior is often so negative that the misunderstanding and disconnection that results causes discord and distress.

3. History of depression. Some partners bring to their marriage a history of their own depression, or a family history that makes them vulnerable to repeated bouts of depression. This has a tendency to build the marriage on a depressive foundation. Research shows that depression is "catching" and that depression in one family member can affect the overall quality of the couple's interaction.

4. Devastating loss. Depression can be the result of suffering a devastating loss such as the loss of love, the loss of a job or reputation, the death of a family member, rejection, divorce, or moving to live in a new neighbourhood.

5. Personality issues. Not knowing how to deal with moodiness, dependency needs, anger cycles, or the withdrawal and unresponsiveness of a partner who is not highly invested in the relationship, can also cause depression in the other partner or in the marriage relationship.

6. Gender differences. Studies show that women tend to experience depression twice as frequently as men and that social and cultural expectations lead to a lack of clarity about roles in relationships that leaves couples, especially women, frustrated, dissatisfied, and even depressed. This ambiguity is a high risk factor for depression in marriage. Relationships that are damaging or emotionally limiting tend to generate very negative feelings, and women who feel hurt, victimized, or who have lost their voice in the relationship are most likely to experience depression. Overall, the most common cause of depression for women occurs as a result of disruption in their closest relationships, while for men the greatest cause of depression is when their self-esteem and status is threatened.

7. Social isolation. Losing a sense of closeness with another person is a trigger for most people to feel lonely and rejected. Depression is far more likely to surface in marriage when someone feels isolated and that they are facing their problems all alone.

8. Boredom. Couples allow their relationship to get locked into a routine that is uninteresting, devitalized, boring, and depressing.

9. Resentment. When couples refuse to acknowledge or express their anger, they often end up turning their feelings of anger inward, and their depression serves to pay back their partner through passive-aggressive behaviors and the withholding of responses that are important to them.[37]

10. Rumination. Another core element of depression is related to the despair generated when an individual's thoughts continue to spin around, becoming increasingly blown out of proportion to the real issues at hand.

11. An imbalance in brain chemistry. Depression can result from changes in the chemistry of the brain or an imbalance in the body's hormones. It can be related to certain physical illnesses (e.g.: diabetes, hypoglycemia), alcohol, drugs, or certain prescribed medications. Women can also experience symptoms of depression associated with premenstrual syndrome or the "postpartum blues" that accompany the birth of a baby, when hormone levels fall dramatically.

Understanding Depression

Depression is a common disturbance that alters and disrupts an individual's moods, thoughts, body, and behavior and is evidenced by feelings of sadness, disappointment, grief, and loneliness. It manifests itself though a variety of emotions experienced on a continuum that ranges from a mild case of "the blues" to a full-blown case of clinical depression. The four common features of depression are:[38] a negative attitude toward self and the future, misery and self-pity, feelings of helplessness and powerlessness, and a sense of futility and apathy.

Awareness of the four major types of depressive illnesses that can seriously affect their relationship can be helpful for couples to know, especially if they are struggling with mood disorders in their marriage. These four types are:

1. Reactive depression—a mild to severe reaction to a distressing life situation (e.g.: loss of job or close relationship).

2. Chronic depression—a longstanding depressive mood owing to an inability to cope with stress, low self-esteem, or unhelpful childhood attitudes or beliefs that leave a person feeling helpless and pessimistic.

3. Endogenous depression—a severe type of depression associated with a chemical imbalance in the brain. While this type of depression may have no obvious triggers, many believe that in addition to biochemical changes, unresolved problems and a build-up of stress also contribute to its presence.

4. Bipolar disorder. Individuals with manic-depressive illness swing from the lows of depression to exaggerated highs that are full of energy, excitement, and euphoria. When either not treated or under treated, it can lead to a much more debilitating condition.

Managing Depression

When one or both partners experience depression, it is imperative that couples seek professional help. Because of the many medical conditions that can cause feelings of depression, having a thorough physical examination by your doctor when symptoms of depression originally become evident is the first step to receiving the proper help needed to treat this significant emotional obstacle to relational health and well-being. Hartin suggests that individuals struggling with depression also take the initiative to do five positive things that will help them combat their depression.[9]

▶ Stop running yourself down.

▶ Stop apologizing for yourself.

▶ Stop blaming yourself and reinforcing the belief that you are bad and responsible for everything.

▶ Finish things, and feel a sense of success and accomplishment.

▶ Do something about your isolation.

Living with someone who is depressed can be very difficult and confusing. The messages you receive can often be quite hurtful and inconsistent, sometimes suggesting blame and hostility, while at other times expressing dependency and despair. If your partner is depressed for any length of time, you may end up feeling frustrated, angry, lost, and afraid. You may long for the person that was and resent what they have now become; you may feel shut out, guilty, and alone, drained, desperate to connect, and willing to do anything to help.[40] At first, you may disregard the signs and become involved in either rationalizing the problem away or simply denying that it is happening.

What can you do? Susan Tanner and Jillian Ball offer ten helpful hints on how to live with someone who is depressed:[41]

1. Validate the depressed partner's feelings. Do not belittle or question whether their depression is real or not. Accept their emotional pain.

2. Relate to the person, not their depression. The person does not become their depression. Connect with them, and separate the person from the problem.

3. Communicate effectively by patiently listening and showing genuine interest. Be empathic and reflective of their feelings, and try to take responsibility for your own feelings by using "I" statements.

4. Give positive messages of affirmation and encouragement. Depressed people often lose confidence in themselves, their judgment, and their ability to make decisions.

5. Help them make decisions, not by directly advising, but by exploring options and helping them to choose their own course of action.

6. Clarify how you can help. When they are feeling reasonably well, discuss in specific terms what they would find helpful if and when they feel "down" again.

7. Learn how to ask a depressed partner to change their behavior. A failure to express your concerns and instead bottle up your feelings only increases your anger over your partner's depressive mood or their behavior. Be assertive, and describe the behavior you wish to see changed, express how you feel about it, specify the required changes, and comment on the consequences.

8. Eliminate unhelpful expectations that may contribute to maintaining the depression in your partner.

9. Establish your own support. You need sometimes to pursue your own needs and interests. You cannot always be caring and giving. You need breaks in order to replenish your own emotional needs.

11. Watch for thoughts of suicide. Depressed partners may be distressed to the point of wanting to end their own lives. Talk to your partner about their thoughts and intentions, validate their fears and feelings for what they are, and open up the possibility of receiving professional help to deal with these issues.

Of all the experiences we regularly encounter in marriage, none can be more difficult and distressing than dealing with anger, stress, and depression. The presence of these negative emotional experiences comprise the core obstacles to success, satisfaction, and happiness in marriage. Learning how to identify and manage them in positive, constructive ways enables couples to find the closeness and intimacy they desire and hunger for in their relationship.

Notes:

1. Karen Prager, "The Intimacy Dilemma," in *The Intimate Couple,* edited by Jon Carlson and Len Sperry (Philadelphia: Brunner/Mazel, 1999), p. 109.

2. Richard S. Lazarus, *Stress and Emotion* (New York: Springer Publishing Company, 1999), pp. 27, 30.

3. Ibid.

4. Mark A. Whisman, "Satisfaction in Close Relationships: Challenges for the 21st Century," in *Satisfaction in Close Relationships*, edited by Robert Sternberg and Mahzad Hojjat (New York: Guilford Press, 1997), p. 398.

5. Andrew Christensen and Pamela T. Walczynski, "Conflict and Satisfaction in Couples," in *Satisfaction in Close Relationships,* edited by Robert Sternberg and Mahzad Hojjat (New York: Guilford Press, 1997), pp. 261, 262.

6. Carlos Durana, "Integrated Psychoeducational Approach," in *The Intimate Couple,* edited by Jon Carlson and Len Sperry (Philadelphia: Brunner/Mazel, 1999), p. 348.

7. Karen Prager, "The Intimacy Dilemma," in *The Intimate Couple,* edited by Jon Carlson and Len Sperry (Philadelphia: Brunner/Mazel, 1999), p. 110.

8. Dolores Curran, *Stress and the Healthy Family* (New York: Harper Collins Publishers, 1987), p. 20.

9. David Olso and Hamilton McCubbin, *Families: What Makes Them Work?* (California: Sage Publications, 1983), p. 21.

10. Dolores Curran, *Stress and the Healthy Family*, pp. 12, 13.

11. Dorothy E. Peven and Bernard H Shulman, "The Issue of Intimacy in Marriage," in *The Intimate Couple*, edited by Jon Carlsen and Len Sperry (Philadelphia: Brunner/Mazel, 1999), p. 283.

12. Warwick Hartin, *For Better For Worse For Ever?* (Victoria, Australia: Thomas C. Lothian Pty, Ltd., 1995), p. 99.

13. David W. Augsburger, *Anger and Assertiveness in Pastoral Care* (Philadelphia: Fortress Press, 1979), p. 71.

14. Mark P. Cosgrove, *Counseling for Anger* (Dallas: Word Publishing, 1988), pp. 27-33.

15. Ibid., p. 27.

16. Clifford I. Notarius, Samuel Lashley, and Debra Sullivan, "Anger and Your Partner: Think Again," in *Satisfaction in Close Relationships,* edited by Robert Sternberg and Mahzad Hojjat (New York: Guilford Press, 1997), p. 221.

17. Mark P. Cosgrove, *Counseling for Anger*, p. 34.

18. Ron Potter-Efron and Pat Potter-Efron, *Letting Go of Anger* (California: New Harbinger Publications, 1995), p. 3.

19. John M. Gottman, *The Marriage Clinic* (New York: W.W. Norton and Company, 1999), p. 12.

20. John M. Gottman, *Why Marriages Succeed or Fail* (New York: Simon and Schuster, 1994), p. 58.

21. John M. Gottman, *Why Marriages Succeed or Fail*, pp. 308, 319.

22. Archibald D. Hart, *Unlocking the Mystery of Your Emotion* (Dallas: Word Publishing, 1989), p. 44.

23. Melvyn L. Fein, *Intergratred Anger Management* (Connecticut: Praeger Publishers, 1993), pp. 19-21.

24. Ibid., pp. 46-55.

25. Clifford I. Notarius, Samuel Lashley, and Debra Sullivan, "Anger

and Your Partner: Think Again," in *Satisfaction in Close Relationships*, p. 276.

26. David Mace and Vera Mace, *Love and Anger in Marriage* (Great Britain: Pickering and Inglis, 1983), p. 18.

27. Bonnie Maslin, *The Angry Marriage* (New York: Skylight Press, 1994), p. 32.

28. Carol Tavris, *Anger, the Misunderstood Emotion* (New York: Simon and Schuster, 1989), pp. 243, 249.

29. Melvyn L. Fein, *Integrated Anger Management*, pp. 11, 12.

30. Carol Tavris, *Anger, the Misunderstood Emotion*, p. 248.

31. Ibid., p. 249.

32. Sharon Wegscheider-Cruse, *Coupleship* (Florida: Health Communications, Inc., 1988), p. 111.

33. Carlfred Broderick, *Couples* (New York: Simon and Schuster, 1979), pp. 107-117.

34. David W. Augsburger, *Helping People Forgive* (Kentucky: Westminster John Knox Press, 1996), p. 61.

35. Jack Dominian, *Marriage* (London: Heinemann, 1995), p. 193.

36. Michael D. Yapko, *Hand-Me-Down Blues* (New York: Golden Books, 1999), p. 131.

37. Carlfred Broderick, *Couples*, p. 137.

38. Warwick Hartin, *For Better For Worse For Ever?*, p. 139.

39. Ibid., pp. 147, 148.

40. Mitch Golant and Susan K. Golant, *What to Do When Someone You Love Is Depressed* (New York: Henry Holt and Company, 1996), p. 3.

41. Susan Tanner and Jillian Ball, *Beating the Blues* (Sydney: Doubleday, 1989), pp. 151-159.

SEVEN

Preventing Marital Breakdown

When two people fall in love and get married, they enter into an intimate relationship that holds out to them the promise of relational satisfaction and happiness that is supposed to last a lifetime ("till death do us part"). In the euphoria of those early days, couples quickly discover just how extremely vulnerable they are to each other. Within the privacy and intimacy of their relationship, they unleash on each other a range of powerful emotional forces that generate more love and enjoyment, and more hurt and hatred, than exists in any other human relationship. A relationship that begins with so much promise and potential can so quickly end up being a disappointment and a disaster. Erich Fromm, in his classic 1956 treatise *The Art of Loving*, commented so aptly on this dilemma when he said that "there is hardly any activity, any enterprise, which is started with such tremendous hopes and expectations, and which fails so regularly, as love."

The myth of the ideal marriage in which two people live "happily ever after" is still a central notion in our thinking about marriage today. Many people assume that being in love and married is a sure way to find emotional and sexual fulfilment and enjoy a relationship that guarantees companionship and friendship. However, what the myth makers fail to tell us is that once the infatuation wears off, such aspirations become more difficult to achieve, and it is not long before disillusionment and despair begin to set

183

in. Only then do we realize the depth of our dilemma and the futility of continuing to believe that relationships are held together solely by romantic love.

The Loss of Intimacy

In reality, a happy, stable marital relationship is not built on the myth of romantic love but on intimacy and understanding. Marriage partners become involved in a dynamic, interactional process that draws them together into a relationship in which they both take responsibility for actively meeting each other's needs and resolving the various problems and differences that emerge as they share life together. Through this process, they achieve a sense of mutual love, acceptance, and intimacy.

Many couples, however, find themselves totally unprepared to deal with the conflicts and problems that gradually begin to accumulate in their marriage. Without knowing exactly what the problem is, they become aware of a growing sense of frustration and hurt and a deepening sense of unrest over their loss of intimacy and understanding. As their relationship becomes overwhelmed with feelings of disappointment, deflation, and defeat, the couple begins to think of their marriage as a big mistake. The feelings of trust, the sense of well-being, the illusion of oneness, are shattered, and their woundedness steers them away from intimate connection.

Aaron Beck, in his book *Love Is Never Enough,* suggests that although love is a powerful emotional force that motivates couples to help and support each other, it is not sufficient in itself to create the substance of an intimate relationship or the personal qualities and skills that are crucial for sustaining and growing a happy, healthy relationship.[1] Other researchers agree. Intimacy can so easily be lost if couples do not have the ability to maintain a sense of openness, affirmation, and positivity in their relationship. Cusinato and L'Abate assert that the major prerequisite for achieving marital intimacy is a healthy, functioning relationship in which couples exercise two sets of abilities:

1. The ability to love and be intimate—which is demonstrated by (a) the degree to which they are emotionally close and available to each other—especially when things get tough—and (b) the amount of importance attributed by both partners to each other and to their relationship.

2. The ability to negotiate—which covers the way they control their emotionality, resolve their differences and problems, and make decisions.[2]

Couples need to know that intimacy in marriage is not an instantaneous process. While some couples can connect with each other immediately, most usually take years to develop a sense of closeness and understanding. For some, intimacy may ebb and flow over time but never really be fully realized in the relationship. For others, it may stand as a solid foundation regardless of life's struggles. Clearly, there is no single or easy path to building on intimate relationship.[3]

Research indicates that couples who are successful in building and sustaining a healthy, functional relationship do so through a process of personal growth, mutual negotiation, and accommodation. However, when there is a discrepancy in the intimacy levels of each partner, or when couples are in conflict about the level of intimacy they each experience or expect to experience, and they cannot negotiate or even talk about it, these discrepancies are particularly destructive to the marriage relationship.[4] Their failure to communicate, make connection, and develop a sense of intimacy creates a feeling of fear that the relationship is in danger of fragmenting and possibly disintegrating. This in itself can become a powerful deterrent that blocks and inhibits further efforts to establish intimacy. The sense of vulnerability created by being close becomes increasingly scary!

Learning to Cope With Growth and Change

It must also be remembered that one of the major challenges facing marital couples is knowing how to balance their needs with the needs of their partner and negotiate their way through the many changes that occur in their relationship over time. Marriage as a relationship is constantly evolving—it is never static. Individual

Year of Marriage	Stage of Marriage	Issues or Tasks in Marriage
0-2	Romantic Stage (Starting Up)	1. Develop "togetherness in marriage" 2. Establish trust and identity 3. Differentiate from family of origin 4. Idealization/Fantasy of romantic love
2-4	Expectations Stage (Settling Down)	1. Resolving Dependency Needs 2. Issue of Power and Control 3. Tolerance of Differences 4. Inclusion/Exclusion
5-6	Power Struggle Stage (Decision Time)	1. Disillusionment/Disenchantment 2. Conflict over differentness 3. Unearthing hidden contracts in Marriage 4. Need to childproof the Marriage
7-15	Reconciliation Stage (Moving On)	1. Recommitment to the Marriage 2. Conflict and competition of Parenting 3. Resolving Anger, practicing Forgiveness 4. Maintain Intimacy
16-24	Redefinition Stage (Mid-life/Adolescent)	1. Flexible Family Boundaries 2. Adolescent Independence 3. Mid-life Issues—self-esteem, competency, new roles, expectations 4. Life cycle parallels—parents and adolescents
25-35	Launching Stage	1. Dealing with disability, grief, and loss 2. Realign adult relationships 3. Resolution versus stagnation 4. Reestablish intimacy
36+	Acceptance Stage	1. Preparing for Retirement 2. Intimacy—renewing love 3. Resignation/Acceptance

Table 7: The Marital Life Cycle

Adapted from Kovac's Marital Development Diagram published in *Psychology Today*, Jan.-Feb. 1992.

partners are confronted with changes in roles, tasks, ambitions, and expectations that can be resisted as stressful, negative, and unwelcome—or embraced as opportunities for growth and development. Learning how to cope with these changes and negotiate their way through the developmental stages of the marital life cycle probably becomes the most significant challenge any marital couple faces.

A significant way to prevent the breakdown of relationships and enhance the potential for intimacy and understanding between couples is for them to know about the various stages of the marital life cycle and those tasks and issues that need to be resolved at each stage. A brief summary of the seven stages of this developmental process is outlined in Table 7 (facing page). Many studies have confirmed that these developmental issues affect marital intimacy by forcing couples, through the process of interaction, accommodation, and acculturation, to develop their own marital system with clearly established structures, roles, norms, language, and a balance of power. If they are not successful in negotiating these issues, intimacy is lost or made more difficult to achieve.

At each stage of the life cycle, couples are required to work out not only mutually acceptable solutions to the various challenges of living together but a range of individual and relational tasks that significantly influence their own health and happiness and that of their relationship. Those tasks that individuals need to resolve in order to achieve intimacy with the partner include:[5]

1. Establishing a positive "emotional comfort zone" or relational climate that is not constantly being contaminated by conflict resurrected and reactivated from experiences with early childhood figures. A healthy differentiation from one's family of origin is a crucial step toward developing the maturity to form intimate relations based on a balance between mutuality and interdependence.

2. Creating and maintaining clear and appropriate personal and interpersonal boundaries that allow for privacy, personal integrity, and free-flowing communication that recognizes the feelings and needs of the partner, encourages self-disclosure, and develops feelings of trust and respect. These boundaries should not be overly rigid (they inhibit growth and devitalize the relationship) or excessively flexible (they create chaos and the fear of dissolution).

3. Developing compatible problem-solving styles that sustain a functional relationship by dealing promptly with frustration, anger, and withdrawal; avoiding the use of aversive tactics; and using defensiveness as an opportunity for clarification and deeper intimacy.

4. Constructing a joint view of social reality that exposes the process of idealization and brings a sense of realism to the relationship. Individuals also need to develop a sense of congruence about how they see themselves and how their partner sees them, so that the potential for tension, conflict, and miscommunication is reduced.

5. Maintaining a sense of passion and companionship through pleasurable events, mutual interests, enjoyment, and novelty. Part of the process of maintaining companionship also involves the mutual commitment of the couple to the relationship and to each other, which is demonstrated through their material and emotional investment in marriage. Sexuality also plays a unique role in maintaining and enhancing a sense of emotional closeness.

In their book *In Quest of the Mythical Mate,* Bader and Pearson suggest that the reason so many couples become bewildered, disillusioned, and even defeated in their quest for intimacy is that they never progress beyond the original fantasy of romantic intimacy (a symbiotic relationship) established in the early years of marriage.

They contend that genuine feelings of closeness, connection, and intimacy only develop as individuals are better able to define themselves and their inner feelings and make a clear separation (differentiation) between themselves and their partner. If individuals do not transition beyond symbiosis, they get entrenched in circular, nonproductive patterns that tend to result in couples being caught in either a conflict-avoidant or a conflict-dominated relationship. Those couples who end up in these relationships tend to sacrifice their own development for the maintenance of the partnership.

Bader and Pearson believe that the transition from symbiosis to differentiation is the most difficult transition of all for most couples to make. The symbiotic stage, which is normal in the early stages of marriage and strongly maintained by cultural and individual beliefs, eliminates the anxiety of being psychologically alone in the world and makes the attainment of intimacy at that stage effortless.

However, while this initial stage gets the relationship started, it is not the foundation for the hard work of sustained intimacy and individual growth. Defining the self, activating the self, establishing and maintaining one's own boundaries, managing the anxiety that comes from risking loss (separation), and achieving greater closeness (intimacy) requires a healthy differentiation. This differentiation enables individuals to explore, appreciate, and persevere in managing contradictions within themselves and differences with and from their partner, and using the discomfort of anxiety for emotional growth.[7]

The point is that while couples may have the ability to love and be intimate with each other, they will find it difficult to sustain and deepen their sense of intimacy in the long term without the ability to negotiate their differences and adapt to the changes that occur over the life cycle of the marriage. When negativity overwhelms a couple and they lose connection with one another, the level of their marital satisfaction declines, and intimacy becomes elusive.

Couples who become distressed by their lack of connection and the loss of intimacy in the marriage will typically engage each other in aversive tactics such as threatening, blaming, or withdrawing as a means of eliciting attention or compliance from their partner.[8] If these tactics fail, marital partners often find themselves stuck in a relationship that is drifting or stagnant. They may even attempt to find expression for their disillusionment and disappointment outside the marriage.

Signs of a Marriage in Trouble

Researchers have consistently found that the level of marital satisfaction declines steadily across the early years of a couple's relationship, finding its lowest level during the adolescent years of the family life cycle (see Figure 9, below). Although this decline may coincide with particular periods in the life cycle, Clements and Markman have suggested that marital satisfaction is better explained by the way partners interact with and treat each other. They propose a theory of relationship distress called the "erosion theory," which assumes that the relatively high degrees of positive factors such as attraction, love, commitment, trust, friendship, and intimacy that exist at the beginning of a relationship gradually erode over time as couples experience conflict and disagreement.

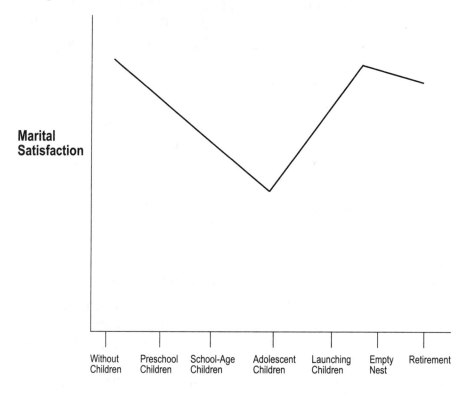

Figure 9: Marriage Satisfaction Across the Marriage Life Cycle

The key to improving marital satisfaction and preventing marital breakdown and burnout is to educate and help couples regulate their negative emotions and find ways to eliminate dysfunctional and destructive interactional patterns. Many couples need help to recognize the signs that they are getting into trouble when their anxiety level begins to rise because they are not connecting with or understanding their partner. Frequently, they just drift into nagging, griping, and fighting with each other without realizing how their negativity is eroding the positive factors that feed the health of their relationship.

Many marriages break down and end in divorce because people do not recognize the early warning signs that the marriage is in trouble. The most common warning signs that emotional distance is developing in a marriage have been identified as:

1. Complaints of loss of feeling. It is quite common for one or both partners to complain that they no longer are in love with the other partner. Frequently, this loss of feeling is related to the fact that their anxiety and fears have been "bottled up" and not expressed—or feelings of resentment, bitterness, and hatred have been harbored by one against the other.

2. Recurring arguments that are not resolved. The research of Gottman, Markman, and others clearly underscores the damaging effects that negativity and recurring patterns of conflict have on a marital relationship.

3. Loss of interest in sex. Sex provides a useful barometer for the relative health of—and/or dysfunction in—a marriage. Couples typically will show a lack of interest in or attraction to each other, when they don't feel emotionally close to one another.

4. Signs of depression or withdrawal by one of the partners. Feelings of dissatisfaction, unhappiness, and helplessness, or a fear of losing the relationship, may cause one of the partners to withdraw and become depressed. A lack of sympathetic attention may account for the loss of enthusiasm and optimism in a marriage, more than being stressed or over-worked.[10]

5. The abandonment of joint activities. Where partners begin to live parallel lives, there is little opportunity for them to spend time together or share in pleasurable activities that increase feelings of attachment and bonding.

6. An affair. Becoming emotionally and sexually involved with someone outside the marriage can be a "cry for help" and a plea for both partners to acknowledge that the relationship is floundering and in trouble.

7. Preoccupation with interests and activities outside the marriage. The investment of time and energy by one partner in career, work, church, or other interests and activities may leave the other partner feeling neglected and betrayed.

8. Arguments over child-rearing. Another significant warning sign is when fights erupt that divide the couple over their methods and commitment to rearing children. These disruptions can sometimes lead individual parents to form an alliance with one or a number of the children against the other partner.

9. Increased fatigue and the reduced ability to meet responsibilities at work. This may signal that a lot of emotional energy is being expended on negative relational issues.

When a marriage is in difficulty, these early warning signs are usually accompanied by other issues that constitute serious barriers to intimacy. Some of these barriers include:

A fear of closeness. An individual finds it hard to share openly their thoughts and feelings with their partner. Having never learned to own their own feelings, they find it hard to get emotionally close, for fear of being hurt. So they play it safe and keep their distance.

Unresolved anger. Carrying around a load of unresolved hurt, anger, grief, or personal issues that have not been resolved will eventually erode intimacy. The mismanagement of anger is probably the greatest single barrier to intimacy in any relationship.

The need for power and control. Partners who are rigid, inflexible, and controlling often manipulate things to stop them from getting out of control, thus making them feel threatened, uncomfortable, or vulnerable.

Low self-esteem. A partner who feels inferior or worthless does not contribute much positive energy to the relationship. The fact that they are often tentative, uncertain, or negative and find it hard to take initiatives with their partner can seriously affect the relationship. Most marriages find it hard to carry an emotionally hurting or wounded person for very long. Frequently this burden creates feelings of resentment in the other partner.

Jealousy and mistrust. Constantly doubting your partner or questioning their love and acceptance seriously undermines trust and confidence in the relationship. Sexual jealousy—which arises from the fear of loss and exclusion and involves feelings of anger, anxiety, and resentment—is particularly distressing, because it threatens the security of the marriage and blocks intimacy.

Idealization of the relationship. Couples who lack a sense of realism about their relationship and hang on to romantic notions of love frequently expect unattainable standards and demand levels of intimacy and togetherness that stifle the relationship and create feelings of frustration and alienation.

Marital Burnout

Ayalo Pines contends that romantic notions of love fostered by our culture set the stage for the eventual burnout of a marriage. Burnout, she says, is the psychological price many are paying for having expected too much from their marriage relationship—an affliction that results when people expect that romantic love will give meaning to their lives and provide the answer to the problems of their human existence. Burnout occurs when an individual finally realizes that despite all their efforts, their relationship does not and will not meet all their needs—or that their partner's love will not bring them complete fulfilment.[11]

Burnout, however, is not inevitable. Many marriages may end up being uncomfortable, devitalized, and unsatisfying without being burned out. In most cases, couples will find a way to live with their differences and realistically accept that marriage is only one of a number of significant factors that contribute to their happiness and fulfilment.

When burnout does occur, it is usually the result of a slow and gradual process best described as a state of physical, emotional, and mental exhaustion.[12] The feelings of exhaustion typically result from conflicting demands constantly to prove oneself, a role overload beyond the point of endurance, and the pressure of unsuccessfully balancing family and work commitments. Of note is that all three of these factors reflect a significant drain of energy, a sense of failure to perform to some expected standard, and an overwhelming feeling of exhaustion that causes an individual to feel so disillusioned and disappointed with their marriage that they cannot cope any longer.

Marital burnout begins to occur when love fades and one or both of the partners have feelings of emotional depletion, hopelessness about the future, and helplessness to do anything about making things better in the marriage.[13] There comes a point beyond which endurance, communication, and coping with the petty annoyances, demands, and shattered expectations of the marriage are no longer desired or sought. Stagnation sets in, and intimacy is blocked. For many couples it is so easy to drift along, doing the same old things and remaining stuck in the same old negative cycles.

On the other hand, burnout may represent a positive turning point. It can serve as a signal to the couple that the marriage is struggling and that the way they feel about themselves and their future provides them with an opportunity to reassess what they really want from each other. It may also help to decide whether they are prepared to leave behind the dead or dying relationship and move on to creating a new and different marriage that works.

Common Causes of Marriage Breakdown

Recent studies in Australia have shown that five years after the breakup of their marriage, 40 percent of individuals said they wished their divorce had never happened. They believed that it could have been avoided had they only recognized the warning signs that their relationship was in trouble. When couples see the signs that indicate that their relationship is struggling or "stuck" and are informed about the causes of their marital breakdown, they are better equipped to avoid their dysfunctional attitudes and behaviors and thus prevent the meltdown of their marriage. The eight main causes of marital breakdown are:

1. Low commitment to the marriage. When couples get married, they make a commitment to three things—their partner, the relationship, and a belief in the permanence of marriage as a covenant relationship. If they are not totally committed in all three areas, the relationship will suffer. When individuals over-commit themselves to work or church, or go after other things like sports or friends, and are not totally invested in making the marriage their number one priority, emotional distance, mistrust, and feelings of betrayal begin to emerge.

The conditions under which the marriage was first established may also undermine commitment to the marriage. If couples are immature and marry too young, if they carry a lot of unresolved issues from their family of origin, or if they get married for all the wrong reasons (e.g.: to escape, to avoid loneliness, because of social pressures, or pregnancy), these can affect the level of bonding and commitment necessary for a stable relationship.

2. Unrealistic expectations. We have already commented on how an idealized image of what the relationship should be can undermine genuine connection and relational growth. When couples collude to avoid facing their differences, they maintain the myth of oneness that negates a balance between connectedness and separateness.

3. Boredom. A great tendency exists for couples to take their partner for granted and become complacent about their relationship. Complacency is one of the deadliest enemies of love. So too, self-absorption, neglect, and condescension are insidious ways of undermining love.[14] When one person drifts along and refuses to confront these attitudes, their partner frequently ends up being bored and losing interest in the relationship.

4. Interpersonal incompetence. A happy marriage depends on two people having the skills to communicate effectively with each other and negotiate their way out of difficulties. Partners with low self-esteem or little or no assertiveness skill cannot contribute strongly and positively to the relationship and often fail to get what they need from the marriage. The lack of ability to deal with jealousy, in-laws, finances, and sexuality often debilitate a relationship and rob it of its energy and its health. Some marital partners who feel inadequate or cannot face the responsibility of sustaining the relationship resort to abusive and/or addictive behaviors rather than developing the personal skills necessary for marital growth. These behaviors traditionally have been very destructive to a marriage.

5. An affair. Up to 25 percent of marriages end because of an affair by one of the partners. Many factors can push or pull individuals toward marital infidelity—attraction, novelty, excitement, risk, challenge, curiosity, enhancing self-esteem, a desire to escape or find relief from a painful relationship, boredom, feeling neglected, a desire to prove one's worth or attractiveness, a desire for attention, or a desire to punish a partner. Research shows that working couples are at greater risk of having affairs than any other group.[15]

6. A developmental or situational crisis. Many marriages do not survive the emotional onslaught that occurs when crisis situations devastate a couple's relationship. Situational crises such as illness, death, or serious accidents to a partner or family member, depression, unemployment, or bankruptcy are difficult events to survive for many couples. Dealing with the crises that occur during the normal developmental stages of the family cycle (e.g.: having children, parenting teenagers, dealing with mid-life) can also destabilize a marriage and cause it to flounder and break up.

7. An imbalance in the relationship. As a marriage relationship grows and changes, the balance of power shifts, causing couples to realign their roles and responsibilities. Marriages can see-saw out of control when issues arise such as educational inequality, personal dominance and control, differences in earning capacity, a wife returning to the workforce and becoming more economically independent, or an imbalance in the power and decision-making process within the couple's relationship.

8. Poor communication. Many marriages break down because of poor verbal and nonverbal communication. Couples who indulge in using vague and unclear ways of communicating and who speak indirectly to each other as a way of avoiding closeness and conflict set the stage to misunderstanding, frustration, and hurt. A survey by the Australian Institute of Family Studies in 1993 found that 70 percent of people surveyed whose marriages had fallen apart nominated lack of communication and the resultant lack of companionship, love, and affection as a the major cause of their relationship failure.

For marriages to survive, couples need to be able not only to love each other and negotiate a resolution of their personal differences, but they must be willing to adapt to the many demands and challenges that impact their relationship both from within and without. At each phase of the marital life cycle, potential exists for either acting-out behaviors or a mutual resolution of relational difficulties and challenges. Being aware of all the issues we have explored in this chapter can help a couple prevent the burnout or meltdown of their marriage and enable them to see and read the signs that point the way down the pathway to mutual love and intimacy.

Notes:

1. Aaron T. Beck, *Love Is Never Enough* (New York: Harper & Row, 1988), pp. 3, 4.

2. Susan M. Johnson and Leslie Greenberg, *The Heart of the Matter* (New York: Brunner/Mazel, 1994), pp. 109, 110.

3. Ibid., p. 121.

4. Karen J. Prager, *The Psychology of Intimacy* (New York: Guilford Press, 1995), pp. 259, 261.

5. Philip M. Brown, *The Death of Intimacy* (New York: Haworth Press, 1995, pp. 137-162.

6. Ellyn Bader and Peter Pearson, "Searching for the Mythical Mate," in *The Intimate Couple,* edited by Jon Carlson and Len Sperry

(Philadelphia: Brunner/Mazel, 1999), pp. 382-384.

7. Ibid., pp. 385, 386.

8. Philip M. Brown, *The Death of Intimacy*, p. 163.

9. Mari L. Clements, Allan Cordova, Howard Markman, and Jean-Philippe Laurenceau, "The Erosion of Marital Satisfaction Over Time and How to Prevent It," in *Satisfaction in Close Relationships,* edited by Robert Sternberg and Mahzad Hojjat (New York: Guilford Press, New York, 1997), pp. 339-343.

10. Michael P. Nichols, *The Lost Art of Listening* (New York: Guilford Press, 1995), p. 8.

11. Ayala M. Pines, *Keeping the Spark Alive* (New York: St Martin's Press, 1988), pp. 3-11.

12. Ibid., p. 12.

13. Ibid., p. 4.

14. William Masters, Virginia Johnson, and Robert Kolodny, *Heterosexuality* (New York: Harper Collins Publishers, 1944), p. 15.

15. Margaret Andrews, "Avoiding and Surviving Infidelity," featured in *Threshold,* published by CSME Australia, vol. 64, 2000, p. 8.

EIGHT

How to Keep Love Alive

Without question, intimacy has become one of the real casualties in our post-modern, high-tech culture. To keep love alive and maintain a sense of passion in a relationship requires knowledge, focus, and commitment—and these simply don't come easily these days. In fact, many people have come to view the idea of achieving a happy, intimate marriage with some degree of caution, cynicism, and suspicion. Much of our suspicion is based on the knowledge that "marriage never really delivers on the romantic images we continue in vain to cultivate."[1]

Furthermore, the messages couples receive about the dangers and realities of marriage often come across as negative and discouraging. Marriage is frequently presented as "hard work"— something that requires just too much personal sacrifice and effort. Those contemplating marriage are confronted by statistics showing that almost half of all marriages will fail.

In spite of all our unrealistic expectations and fears, marriage is still very popular. The majority of people who aspire to marital satisfaction and happiness enter the "holy estate of matrimony" with the hope and conviction that intimacy is achievable and that they will be successful in having a happy marriage. They see the marriage relationship as a wonderful way of meeting their personal need for love, friendship, and belonging.

If you ask couples who enjoy a really good marital relationship what they do to make it work, they will probably tell you how much fun they have sharing life with their partner and how they enjoy being cared for by someone whose love, respect, and support delights, affirms, and nourishes them. Others will tell you that all it takes is common sense—just be a decent human being, treat each other well, and try not to fight too much. They make it sound as if there is a set formula that everyone knows innately, and all you have to do is be in love and follow the rules.

Surprisingly, all successful, thriving marriages are different. They don't conform to a set formula or function according to the same pattern. They all reveal a beauty uniquely their own.

Maintaining the Love Relationship

However, we need to recognize that successful marriages are not self-generating. They do not occur spontaneously or by chance. They require a great deal of energy and investment to make them work. To keep love alive and achieve a sense of passion, commitment, and intimacy, good marital relationships require reciprocity.[2] They are the result of an ongoing process of caring and closeness in which two people work together to create an enduring relationship with both partners experiencing increasing fulfilment and satisfaction.

While it is true that many changes in a relationship are inevitable, couples need to recognize that keeping love alive and achieving marital growth is intentional. They can either allow their relationship to change arbitrarily as other circumstances around them are altered, or they can be intentional about making choices that keep the flame of passion and love alive and that facilitate the course of growth in the marriage. Gottman asserts that couples who do nothing wrong but who do nothing to make things better in their marriage will find that their marriage will still tend to get worse over time."[3] He argues that marital couples need to make an effort to implement strategies and behaviors that keep a marriage fresh and alive and help a good relationship get even better.

Dominian believes that marital love implies mutual growth— the ability to accept, change, and grow together by acknowledging each other's reality, by unpacking one another's hidden world, and by demonstrating a capacity to forgive each other for not turning out to be all that was originally projected.[4] He suggests that couples who wish to maintain their marriage in a healthy state need to know how to nurture love over the whole marital life cycle by both *maintaining* and *repairing* their relationship.[5] Maintaining the relationship involves the use of strategies that build togetherness, harmony, warmth, affection, and effective communication. Repair measures refer to any action that prevents negativity from escalating out of control. These actions to repair the relationship, Gottman describes as "the secret weapon of emotionally intelligent couples," because they enable them to strengthen the marriage by over-riding negativity.[6] Markman's approach to marital education, in the PREP program, places a similar emphasis on those core issues that lower the risks of marital conflict and distress (repair) and those measures that raise protection and enhance the relationship (maintenance), such as commitment, friendship, fun, sensuality, spirituality, and religious intimacy.[7]

Keys to Intentional Marital Growth

A massive lack of knowledge exists about what maintains the majority of marital relationships.[8] While we know a great deal about the factors involved in the formation of relationships and a considerable amount about the causes and consequences of relationships that fail and end in dissolution, little research has been carried out to determine the key factors involved in relationship maintenance. Researchers have tended to assume that we can easily understand what these factors are by simply extrapolating from the periods of relationship formation and dissolution.[9] A lot of the material written about how to build intimacy and maintain love relationships typically sets forth a menu or list of dos and don'ts developed from an understanding of what causes marital breakdown—or what factors create obstacles to intimacy in marriage.

Byrne and Murnen strongly reject the idea that maintaining a healthy love relationship involves a simple repetition of those variables that initiated attraction in the early, formative stages of a relationship, or the mere absence of those factors associated with the failure of the relationship.[10] Common sense, for example, would suggest that the absence of bitter arguments and negative interactions does not automatically guarantee marital stability and happiness. Clearly, there is a range of positive measures that couples intentionally use to nurture and maintain their marriage.

Byrne and Murren suggest three realms of interpersonal interactions vital to maintaining or failing to maintain a loving relationship:

1. Similarity of attitudes, values, beliefs, interests, and personality dispositions that create satisfaction and closeness.

2. Habituation. Familiarity and endless repetitions which breed both contempt and boredom, rather than enthusiasm and creativity.

3. Positive evaluations. The use of interpersonal skills to communicate positive feelings that build and encourage closeness and connection.

Byrne and Murren particularly emphasize the proposition "that reciprocal positive evaluative behavior plays a crucial role in maintaining a satisfying and loving relationship. If couples can *reinforce* one another, *interact* gently, and *behave* in ways that please each partner, their relationship should obviously benefit."[11]

Biblical Advice on Maintaining Love Relationships

The New Testament apostles were clear in their instructions to the Christian church about what it takes to keep marriages and relationships alive, healthy, and strong. Their writings suggest a range of attitudes and behaviors designed to maximize the positive (protection measures) and minimize the negative (risk factors). The author of Hebrews suggests that we should "stay on good terms with each other, held together by love" and that we must "honour marriage and guard the sacredness of sexual intimacy between husband and wife" (Hebrews 13:1, 4, *THE MESSAGE*).

The apostle James encourages us to "live well, live wisely, live humbly" (James 3:13, *THE MESSAGE*). It is not the way you talk that counts, he says, but the way you live your life. He goes on to say that the way we treat each other should not be affected by the ebb and flow of how we feel, but by our acknowledgement of God's wise ways.

> Real wisdom begins with a holy life and is characterized by getting along with others. It is gentle and reasonable, over-flowing with mercy and blessings, not hot one day and cold the next, not two faced. You can develop a healthy robust community that lives right with God and enjoys the results only if you do the Lord's work of getting along with each other, treating each other with dignity and honour" (James 3:17, 18, *THE MESSAGE*).

The apostle Paul has much to say about maintaining love and renewing a sense of passion and intimacy in our relationship. These behaviors, he believed, arise out of thankful hearts and lives filled with the grace of God. "Let the peace of Christ keep you in tune with each other, in step with each other" (Colossians 3:15, *THE MESSAGE*).

> Love from the center of who you are; don't fake it...be good friends who love deeply...don't burn out; keep yourselves fu-eled and aflame...laugh with your happy friends when they're happy; share tears when they're down. Get along with each other...don't hit back; discover beauty in everyone" (Romans 12:9-17, *THE MESSAGE*).

Paul further instructs us to "look for the best in each other, and always do our best to bring it out" (1Thessalonians 5:14, *THE MESSAGE*). He encourages us to allow the gifts of God's Spirit— "love, joy, peace, patience, kindness, goodness, faithfulness, gentle-ness and self control" (Galatians 5:22, 23, NIV) to energize our relationship as we pour ourselves "out for each other in acts of love" (Ephesians 4:3, *THE MESSAGE*).

Paul also has some practical counsel for husbands and wives. In

Ephesians 5 (*THE MESSAGE*), he invites couples to "be courteously reverent to one another out of respect for Christ." He obviously sees respect as an important ingredient in building a strong, stable marriage by suggesting here that it is the foundation stone of any successful marriage relationship. Wives, he says, should "understand and support" their husbands, and husbands should "go all out in their love for their wives." A husband should be a source of love and take the lead in cherishing, not dominating, his wife. His love for her is to be a love that is marked by giving, not getting—a love that "brings out the best in her" and "evokes her beauty." The apostle Peter adds to this advice by suggesting that "in the new life of God's grace" couples treat each other as equals, each honoring and delighting in their partner and seeking to be agreeable, sympathetic, loving, compassionate and humble (1 Peter 3:7, 8, *THE MESSAGE*).

The apostles clearly recognize that when couples respect, honor, and support one another, they build a sense of meaning and purpose into their marriage and into their lives. They understood that husbands and wives need to "learn how to love appropriately" (Philippians 1, *THE MESSAGE*) and be intentional about daily renewing a sense of passion and intimacy in their marriage. In this, they see the grace of God empowering and sustaining relationships and intimacy and understanding increasing.

Keeping Love Alive

The early days of marriage are nearly always filled with intoxicating feelings of romance, desire, and passion. These feelings create such an aura of excitement and uncertainty that they greatly enhance a couple's awareness of the intimate experiences they share with their partner. If only they could maintain this level of love, respect, and desire forever!

However, even in the best of marriages, familiarity and predictability come to characterize the relationship more and more as the sense of novelty and the intensity of emotion wear off. Gradually, the excitement and enthusiasm that once stimulated the marriage now begin to decline, and the promises made at the start now begin to fade in importance. Before long, the marriage relationship begins to spiral downward, to the point where the married partners show more honor and respect to friends and strangers than they do to each other. Nothing epitomizes this sad loss of love and romance any better than the classic song, "You Don't Bring Me Flowers," sung by Barbra Streisand and Neil Diamond:

You don't bring me flowers
You don't sing me love songs
You hardly talk to me anymore
When you come through the door
At the end of the day.

I remember when...
You couldn't wait to love me
You used to hate to leave me
Now after lovin' me
It's good for you babe
You're feeling alright
You just roll over and
Turn out the light
And you don't bring me flowers anymore.

Baby I've remembered
All the things you've taught me
I learned how to laugh
And I learned how to cry
Well I learned how to love
And I learned how to lie
So, you think I could learn
How to tell you good-bye
You don't bring me flowers anymore.

The sad thing is that most people have never been taught how to keep love alive. They don't know what it takes to create and maintain a happy, healthy marriage. Often, after years of self-effort, trying hard to please, and stuffing the pain inside, couples start to give up. They find it harder and harder to pretend that they feel the way they really do.

Frequently, when things start to go wrong, couples try to get closer sexually, in the hope they can recapture the feeling of intimacy and closeness. Others may try to talk it out, without realizing that intimacy is an intensely emotional or affective experience that requires more than just words and reasons. Still others will shift their focus away from the relationship to their involvement with their children, career, religion, sports, or other interests.

So what does it take to keep love alive? What are the factors that develop a greater sense of intimacy in marriage? Gottman says that we need to educate couples to *reconcile their conflicts* or differences constructively, *strengthen the positive side of their marriage* and regularly *inoculate their relationship* against the forces that lead to divorce. He believes that happy marriages are based on a deep friendship in which two people mutually respect and enjoy each other's company. These are the couples who know each other intimately, who are well versed in their likes, dislikes, personality quirks, hopes, and dreams, and who have an abiding regard and fondness for each other that is expressed in big and little ways day in and day out.

Ten Qualities That Enhance Intimacy in Marriage

The range of personal and interpersonal qualities, attitudes, and behaviors that researchers highlight as important for maintaining and enhancing intimacy in the marriage relationship vary slightly, depending on their theoretical orientation and focus of investigation. However, these factors are not so dissimilar that they cannot be grouped together in a way that gives us a clear picture of what to do to keep love alive and vibrant and build a greater sense of intimacy in marriage. What follows not only synthesizes most of that research, but it also summarizes all the themes we have highlighted in previous chapters as important issues for developing intimacy in marriage.

1. Goodwill. The first and most important quality for enhancing intimacy in marriage is an attitude of goodwill and cooperation. Displaying goodwill toward your partner is absolutely fundamental to the survival and health of your relationship. Showing your partner goodwill means that you are on their side and just as concerned about meeting their needs as you are your own. It means that your spirits are open to each other and that you have empathy for your partner's point of view. It means demonstrating feelings of fair play and a willingness not to impugn your partner's motives.

Page suggests that goodwill in a relationship incorporates several critical qualities: an attitude of gratitude for each other and for the relationship; mutual acceptance and tolerance; a focus on the positive qualities of the relationship; and self-sacrifice—a willingness to give freely and genuinely of oneself, creating a sense of inter-dependence.[14]

2. Mutual respect and trust. Mutual respect is a central ingredient in all satisfying, long-term marriage relationships. To have respect means to "look at" another and to see what is really there and what potential exists. So to show respect for your partner means that you recognize and accept them as separate individuals and that you value and esteem them for who they are, not for what you can get from them. Showing respect is not the same as romantic admiration, which is based on your idealization of your partner. Respect is clearly about honoring and appreciating your partner's separateness and the ways in which they are unique. It involves valuing their contributions, acknowledging their differences, accepting their needs, and empathizing with their feelings.

Mutual respect in marriage grows as a result of two people moving toward each other with a desire to form a deep union based on accepting and respecting themselves. Couples need to understand that it is very difficult to respect another's feelings, thoughts, actions, individuality, and personality if they do not first respect themselves. Mutual respect can only be achieved when partners set appropriate boundaries, communicate honestly, and seek not to control one another. This separateness is the basis of the couple's relational strength and reduces all "power struggles" in the relationship. Without such reciprocal respect, there cannot be intimacy.[15] Intimacy is usually only achieved when couples show each other an equality of importance and reciprocity of respect.[16]

If two individuals are able to develop a relationship based on mutual respect for each other, a sense of love and trust will begin to emerge. Their trust in each other becomes a critical ingredient in creating emotional safety and fostering true intimacy within their relationship, as the genuine individuality and true selves of each partner blossom and flourish. Being able to trust another person in this way means you have confidence in them not to harm, exploit, deceive, or betray you and that you believe they will respect your intimate disclosures and act in ways that make them worthy of your trust. By communicating openly and honestly, couples develop and nurture a mutual trust that becomes a prized gift and the source of companionship and peace of mind.

When trust is fragile and uncertain, couples tend to hold back on intimacy in order to protect themselves. They find it hard to commit their heart and soul to the marriage relationship or take the risk of being vulnerable to their partner's actions or responses. Couples who do trust each other and invest in one another's good find that they are not easily threatened by disagreements or outbursts of anger and negative feelings, because they feel safe in the relationship and know that such encounters will not destroy their relationship but help it grow and flourish.

3. Effective communication. Social psychologist Elaine Hatfield maintains that intimacy is a process in which a couple attempts to move toward complete communication on all levels, and that the verbal expression of feelings within a relationship becomes the actual bedrock of intimacy.[17] Being able to communicate effectively is probably the most important human survival skill couples have for connecting with each other. Couples who thrive in their marriage relationship indicate that they continue to dialogue with each other through the good times as well as the difficult times in their relationship.

Communicating effectively with each other involves the following skills: being sensitive to and empathizing with your partner's feelings; being able to talk with measured honesty about your own inner experience and feelings; actively listening; speaking and responding nondefensively; being able to validate what you have heard, understood, and accepted as your partner's message; being able to affirm and encourage your partner and demonstrate your affection for them; being assertive and asking for what you want; and being able to share honestly your beliefs, values, difficulties, and accomplishments.

Couples need to remember that emotional expression is a powerful part of intimate communication, because it conveys vulnerability, invites closeness, and, when congruent with nonverbal signs of emotion, conveys genuineness.[18] Without emotional availability, intimacy is superficial and short lived.

4. Mutual commitment. Commitment is the one quality that contributes most to the continuing development of intimacy and growth in marriage. In marriages that last, intimacy and commitment go hand in hand. A lack of commitment on the part of one or both partners is one of the surest and quickest ways of undermining a marriage relationship. Any indication that there may be ambivalence or pretense about one's dedication, loyalty, or faithfulness only creates a sense of uncertainty and insecurity, causing a partner to become preoccupied with concerns about abandonment.

The integrity of any marriage relationship is evidenced by an individual's commitment to the continuing well being of their partner and the relationship and to a belief in the sanctity of marriage that transcends the feelings and considerations of the moment. The reason that mutual commitment has such a powerful effect on a marriage is that it indicates the strength of a partner's investment in the relationship and that they intend to continue in the marriage. It also indicates how much an individual believes in and is committed to the values and goals of their relationship. By the act of commitment, marital partners express their desire to overcome tenaciously their differences and dedicate themselves to building greater intimacy in their relationship by creating new opportunities for deepening love and growing a great friendship.

A variety of ways are available to couples for strengthening their commitment. These include talking more as friends; doing more fun things together; being more forgiving of each other; being less self-centered; expressing positive messages that affirm, encourage, and support each other; making time together a priority; developing a greater sense of teamwork; reaffirming memories of good times shared; talking more openly about plans for the future; and behaving in ways that show faithfulness to the marriage.

5. Expressing appreciation and affection. John Gottman has stressed how important it is for couples consistently to do and say things that give emotional support and provide positive encouragement for their marital partner. Other researchers emphasize that expressions of affection and the free and frequent exchange of tenderness and touch also have a powerful, positive effect on the marital relationship and signify a couple's connectedness and high regard. These caring attitudes and behaviors are vitally important for fueling the sense of romance and passion that keeps the relationship alive and fresh and for creating a sense of playfulness and friendship in the marriage.

Couples who spend time together enjoying leisure activities or who consistently spend quality time with each other tend to promote a greater sense of happiness and marital satisfaction than those who have little time to be together. Couples need to be intentional in promoting their partner's well-being and in improving the sense of bonding, attachment, and intimacy in their relationship, by using the following "minimum daily requirements":

a. Show your partner that you accept their ideas, suggestions, solutions, and feelings.

b. Voice your feelings of love and romantic passion. Say "I love you" at least once a day.

c. Express your appreciation—give compliments and affirmation to your partner at least once a day.

d. Share your feelings. Give your partner one full-bodied hug at least once a day; kiss your partner at least two different ways each day; touch each other tenderly each day to express your love and appreciation.

These "daily" acts of appreciation are part of your "ministry" to your partner and create a sense of intimacy, joy, and delight that enriches your marriage, making it exciting and enjoyable.

6. Be adaptable. Intimacy is very much related to an individual's ability to be open to change and embrace new ideas. The fine art of compromise and the skill of shifting one's attitude or behavior to deal with changing circumstances and to cope with stress or crises are important parts of keeping love alive. Individuals who are rigid and insist on always being right are usually not people who are well loved. This can be particularly true in marriages involving religious couples who become drawn into a belief that there is only one right way to do or see things—and they develop a rigid, dogmatic, inflexible attitude that is destructive to relationships and unforgiving of differences.

Successful couples are also flexible about the roles they play in their relationship. The way they adjust to situations and needs that change over time and the way they handle difficulties as they arise are critical to relational harmony and happiness. In those situations where both partners work outside the home, efforts need to be made to share the workload at home, if misunderstandings are to be avoided. Being adaptable also enables a couple to negotiate ways of working together, assist each other, and build a sense of teamwork and partnership into the marriage.

7. Resolve conflicts. Conflict is the gateway to intimacy. Couples who are willing to face their differences and work through their conflicts to find mutually acceptable solutions to their problems, without being overwhelmed by negative emotions or causing each other to feel angry, criticized, misunderstood, ignored or put down, have found the way to developing a greater sense of understanding and intimacy. While conflict can be a challenge to any relationship, it can also be a creative, growth-producing process that gives people the opportunity to say "I'm sorry" and restore the much-needed equilibrium to their marriage.

Couples need to be shown how to stop recycling their gripes and complaints and share their hurts and fears, admit their errors, and accept their personal limitations, so they can get on with enjoying their relationship together. They also need to get rid of the ghosts of the past—issues that constantly come back to haunt and hurt them and stop them from taking responsibility for their unhappiness and disquiet. Unresolved childhood issues can be very intrusive and destructive in a marriage and need to be addressed. The capacity to give and receive forgiveness for past errors and indiscretions plays a vital role in helping couples to find a resolution to their hurts and pains and to move on in their relationship toward greater intimacy.

8. Sexual satisfaction. Giving expression to sexual passion is a core aspect of marriage and includes a desire for intimacy and closeness, both physically and emotionally. The level of sexual intimacy achieved is itself influenced by the overall state of the relationship and indicates how willing a couple is to respect, trust, and cooperate with each other. When marital partners understand and accommodate each other's sexual needs, their lovemaking activities have the ability to strengthen the bonds of their relationship far beyond the bedroom. Couples who lack the ability to pleasure each other and nurture a sense of spontaneity, curiosity, and playfulness often find that their sex life is unexciting, unsatisfying, and boring, and that the relational bond they experience is diminished. Couples who invest in an imaginative and healthy sex life know that one of the secrets to keeping romance and passion alive is to bring out the attractiveness in each other and give expression to sexual desire. They know, however, that good sex is not a matter of passion and performance but is often a matter of being attuned to their partner's feelings and preferences and knowing when not to do certain things.[19]

9. Spiritual values. Religious and spiritual values play a much more important role in marital stability and happiness than most people realize. The fact is that a couple's spiritual orientation helps them make sense of life and provides meaning and purpose for virtually every aspect of their lives. While a person may be virtuous without being religious, religion does emphasize those qualities most of us would consider virtuous—honesty, integrity, responsibility, commitment, forgiveness, and compassion. Sociologist Andrew Greeley hypothesized that the warmer and more passionate one's religious imaging, the warmer and more passionate one's marriage—and that the higher one's scores on the "grace" scale, the more satisfying and intense the sexual relationship with one's partner is likely to be. He sees a direct correlation between marital intimacy and warm images of God.[20]

10. Social connectedness. Within all human beings is an innate drive to connect with another—a drive crucial to one's esteem and survival. Couples who develop and maintain a healthy relationship with extended family and friends and who feel a part of the wider community in which they live find that this involvement in other relationships typically makes available additional resources that energize and empower their marital relationship, by creating a greater sense of adaptability, tolerance, and openness to sharing. The improvement in self-esteem and relational skills enables couples to pursue and achieve a greater sense of intimacy and connectedness in their own marriage.

Couples who develop these intimate connections with each other are able to maintain a relational bond that grows and strengthens over the life of their marriage. They are able to give and receive love and be affectionate, playful, and adventuresome. They can collaborate, cooperate, negotiate, and communicate in effective ways with each other. These couples are able to soothe, stimulate, touch, hug, hold, gaze, comfort, validate, listen, respond, support, and honor one another and thereby create a safe, secure, emotional environment in which love can flourish. They know the key ingredients that rekindle a sense of romance in their marriage and keep love alive.[21]

Notes:

1. Susan Page, *Now That I'm Married, Why Isn't Everything Perfect* (New York: Bantam Doubleday Dell Publishing Group, Inc.,1994) p. xxii.

2. William Masters, Virginia Johnson, and Robert Kolodny,

Hetrosexuality (New York: Harper Collins Publishing, 1994), p. 15.

3.   John M. Gottman, *Why Marriages Succeed or Fail* (New York: Simon & Schuster, 1994), p. 61.

4.   Jack Dominian, *Marriage* (London: Heinemann, 1995), pp. 114-121.

5.   Ibid., p. 121.

6.   John M. Gottman, *The Seven Principles for Making Marriage Work* (New York: Crown Publishers, Inc., 1999), pp. 22, 23.

7.   Howard Markman, Scott Stanley, and Susan Blumberg, *Fighting for Your Marriage* (San Francisco: Jossey-Bass Publishers, 1994, pp. 119-305.

8.   Jack Dominian, *Marriage,* p. 121.

9.   Donn Byrne and Sarah K. Murnen, "Maintaining Loving Relationships," chapter 13 in *The Psychology of Love,* edited by Robert Sternberg and Michael Barnes (New Haven: Yale University Press, 1988), p. 293.

10.   Ibid., p. 294.

11.   Ibid., pp. 296-302.

12.   John M. Gottman, *Why Marriages Succeed or Fail*, pp. 29, 30.

13.   John M. Gottman, *The Seven Principles for Making Marriage Work,* pp. 19, 20.

14.   John M. Gottman, *The Seven Principles for Making Marriage Work,* pp. 28-47

15.   Susan M. Johnson and Leslie S. Greenberg, *The Heart of the Matter* (New York: Brunner/Mazel, 1994), p. 115.

16.   Ibid., p. 119.

17.   William Masters, Virginia Johnson, and Robert Kolodny, *Heterosexuality*, p. 18.

18.   Jon Carlson and Len Sperry, *The Intimate Couple* (Philadelphia: Brunner/Mazel, 1999), p. 147.

19.   William Masters, Virginia Johnson, and Robert Kolodny, *Heterosexuality,* pp. 17, 18.

20.   Paul Coleman, *The 30 Secrets of Happily Married Couples* (Maryland: Bob Adam, Inc., 1992), pp. 139-141.

21.   Jon Carlson and Len Sperry, *The Intimate Couple*, p. 59.

Conclusion

Throughout the preceding pages, the discussion about intimacy in marriage has focused mainly on the role emotion plays in the bonding process and the affective responses and interactional processes that engage a couple when they fall in love and form a marital relationship. We have not portrayed ways in which emotional connections occur between a man and a woman purely in terms of romantic love, but against the backdrop of Sternberg's definition that sees love as a mutual, experiential journey involving the three components of passion, commitment, and intimacy. These essential elements, when balanced together, provide the basis for a healthy love relationship and a mutually satisfying and fulfilling marriage.

Our discussion began with a survey of the biblical view of marriage growing out of the creative genius and activity of the divine Creator. The Genesis record reveals two distinct views. First, God made men and women for each other, and He did not intend for them to live alone but created marriage as a means for them to enjoy the union of their diverse personalities in love—and to experience a sense of mutuality, satisfaction, and fulfilment through the "oneness" of the marriage relationship. Second, despite our sordid failures in loving and our fearful and self-protective behaviors in living, God has freely offered us His grace and forgiveness to motivate us toward those original ideals, empowering us through His love once again to taste the enjoyment and ecstasy that comes through the intimacy of marriage.

While we have explored the ways in which our expectations of marriage have changed in the face of post-modern thinking, and how many factors conspire to cause the breakdown of the marriage relationship, the major focus of this study has been to highlight those relational skills that couples need to build into their relationship if they are to achieve the goal of intimacy and happiness in marriage. It is our belief that a more focused educational approach is needed to help marital couples and those preparing for marriage to be aware of the emotional issues that significantly impact their marriage in a negative way, as well as the interpersonal skills necessary to find the pathway to resolution when their relationship is deadlocked by difference and negativity. It is also our belief that couples need to be made aware of the many research findings that describe the positive attitudes of healthy couples in long-lasting relationships, and the ways in which they can embrace these attitudes and behaviors and enrich and strengthen their marriage.

Most couples these days are hungry for information on how to make their marriage work. In spite of the fact that the early years of marriage are so often enshrouded in romance and love, couples quickly come to realize just how unprepared they are to face the realities of life together. When the realities of living together and the illusions of romantic love wear off, they begin to search for a better way of understanding how to sustain their love for each other, create a place for healing their sense of woundedness, and grow a satisfying marital relationship.

All of this creates a tremendous challenge for the leaders of the Adventist church and especially for those who minister directly to individuals, couples, and families in the local congregation. It is not that the church has failed to declare its support for marriage or that it has been negligent in upholding the need for couples to remain true and faithful to their wedding vows, but it has shown little initiative in applying the practicalities of the gospel to the actual, living experience of most couples in the church. Some would even suggest that the Adventist church has no business marrying people or even being seen to regulate divorce and re-marriage, without equipping couples with an adequate knowledge of what people should expect to get out of marriage. In this re-gard, there are two pertinent questions that need to be addressed if the ministry of the church is to be relevant and effective.

▶ What is it that people want to get from marriage these days?

▶ What are the main challenges facing the ministry leaders of the church in their work with couples?

What People Want From Marriage

Understanding what people want from marriage may help those who work with couples to focus their efforts on important needs and concerns. Three significant issues motivate people toward marriage today:

1. The need for emotional connection. All couples have a psychological and emotional expectation that their marriage will meet their need for affection, affirmation, and attachment. The process of romantic attachment, which tends to follow the same pattern and process as the early attachment process of child-hood days, meets a basic desire to feel loved, needed, and ap-preciated.

2. A feeling of security and stability. Growing out of the need to be bonded to another significant person who is "there for you" is the psychological and emotional desire for the feeling of per-sonal and relational security. To know and experience that in the midst of change and transition gives one a solid emotional basis for coping with the uncertainties and crises of family life.

3. A desire for sexual intimacy. In order for a couple to avoid feelings of uncertainty, jealousy, or betrayal that can so quickly erode their relationship, they need to know the security and safety that comes from a committed sexual relationship with a partner who is loyal and faithful to the marriage and in no way places at risk the future welfare of their children.

Challenges Facing Ministry Leaders Who Work With Couples

Of all the challenges facing the church in the twenty-first century, none are more important to its future relevance and credibility than the issue of relationships and marriage. Those salient challenges that must be addressed by the church in relation to love and marriage are:

1. What makes marriages work? Positive and practical information needs to be provided to help couples know how to be successful in building a quality marital relationship that enhances satisfaction and builds into it a sense of resilience. The church needs to promote a model of marriage that makes sense to post-modern couples pointing out what it sees as distinctive and important about the marriage relationship. It also needs to promote strategies that prepare, nurture and support couples in the development of the relationship. Specific efforts need to be made to select that information and research that best answers the critical needs of contemporary marriages and shows busy couples how to deal with marriage difficulties and the breakdown of relationships.

2. The need to affirm the role of emotion in marital relationships. Most Christian couples have difficulty understanding the way in which emotion facilitates the powerful bond of attachment that forms between marital partners. The church needs not only to address its attitude toward feelings and emotion but to empower couples to know how to connect at the level of their feelings.

3. An adequate theology of sexuality. The church has a responsibility to uphold a clear, biblical understanding of human sexuality. It needs to put forth greater efforts to educate couples about the way scripture presents conjugal love, sex, and spirituality as part of an integrated whole.

The realities of dealing with the inner world of marriage as described in this book provide a range of material that can be utilized to resource, create, and present a marriage-education program for people at the local congregational or regional level. The aspects of marriage discussed here focus mainly on understanding what intimacy is and how it is achieved, the way that verbal and nonverbal communication is the main vehicle for developing emotional closeness, the importance of sexuality in sustaining and maintaining intimacy, and specific techniques for dealing with conflict and differentness in marriage and overcoming negativity and destructive emotional patterns of interaction.

This material could be organized in many ways and presented to marital or premarital couples in an educational setting. The most effective method of educating couples is one that utilizes both didactic and experiential approaches. A balanced program that allows for couples to receive information, research, and practical suggestions from a group leader needs to be followed by experiential exercises or activities that encourage them to integrate this material into their own lives and practice new relational skills that will enhance the quality of their relationship.

A suggested program for achieving this purpose is outlined below in a series of one-hour sessions.

Session 1: **Warning Signs of a Marriage in Distress** (video)
- Marital Satisfaction Over the Life Cycle
- Evaluating Your Marriage (Dyads)

Session 2: **Intimacy in Marriage**
- Definitions of love and intimacy
- A Biblical view of Marriage (Group Discussion)
- Evaluate your Marriage (Dyads)

Session 3: **Couple Communication**
- Understanding the Communication Process
- Keys to Active Learning (Video)
- Practicing your Listening, Reflecting, and
  Responding Skills (Dyads)

Session 4: **Dealing With Conflict and Anger**
- Understanding Anger as a Secondary Emotion
- A Model for Resolving Conflict and Anger

- Practicing the "Speaker-Listener" Technique (Dyads)
- Resolving Your Conflict Issues (Dyads)

Session 5: **Sexual Satisfaction**
- A Biblical View of Human Sexuality
- Four stages of Arousal (Group Discussion)
- Evaluating your level of Sexual Satisfaction (Dyads)

Session 6: **How to Keep Love Alive**
- Love is not Enough
- Qualities of a Happy Marriage (Group Discussion)
- Contract for Change (Dyads)

Bibliography

Alberti, Robert and Michael Emmons. *Your Perfect Right* (Calif.: Impact Publishers, 1995).

Augsburger, David W. *Helping People Forgive* (Kentucky: Westminster John Knox Press, 1996).

Bristow, John Temple. *Love, Marriage and Family* (Michigan: Chalice Press, 1994).

Brown, Emily M. *Patterns of Infidelity and their Treatment* (New York: Brunner/Mazel, 1997).

Carrell, Brian. *Moving Between Times. Modernity and Post-modernity: A Christian View* (Auckland, NZ: The DeepSight Trust, 1998).

Chapell, Bryan. *Each for the Other: Marriage As It's Meant to Be* (Michigan: Baker Books, 1998).

Curran, Delores. *Stress and the Healthy Family* (San Francisco, Calif.: Harper Collins Publishers, 1985).

Doane, Jeri A. and Diana Diamond. *Affect and Attachment in the Family* (San Francisco, Calif.: Harper Collins Publishers, 1994).

Dominian, Jack. *Marriage* (London: W. Heinemann, Ltd, 1995).

Evatt, Cris. *He and She* (Berkeley, Calif.: Conari Press: Berkeley, 1992).

Faul, John and David Augsburger. *Beyond Assertiveness* (Texas: Word Publishers, 1980).

Frost, Michael. *Longing for Love* (Sydney, AU: Albartross Books, 1996).

Galvin, Kathleen, M. and Bernard Brommel. *Family Communication* (Illinois: Scott, Foresman & Co., 1982).

Gordon, Lori H. *Passage to Intimacy* New York: Simon & Schuster, 1993).

Gottman, John M. and Nan Silver. *The Seven Principles for Making Marriage Work* (New York: Crown Publishers Inc., 1999).

Gottman, John. *Why Marriages Succeed or Fail* (New York: Simon & Schuster, 1994).

Gottman, John. *The Marriage Clinic* (New York: W.W. Norton & Company, 1999).

Hart, Archibald. *Adrenaline and Stress* (Texas: Word Publishing, 1991).

Hart, Archibald. *Me, Myself and I* (Surrey, England: Highland Books, 1992).

Hart, Archibald. *The Sexual Man* (Texas: Word Publishing, 1994).

Heitler, Susan M. *From Conflict to Resolution* (New York: W.W. Norton & Co, 1990).

Johnson, Susan M. and Leslie Greenberg, eds. *The Heart of the Matter: Perspectives on Emotion in Marital Therapy* (New York: Brunner/ Mazel, 1994).

Johnson, Susan, M. *Creating Connection: The Practice of Emotionally Focused Marital Therapy* (New York: Brunner/Mazel, 1996).

Josselson, Ruthellen. *The Space Between Us* (Newbury Park, Calif.: Sage Publishers, 1996).

Lewis, Jerry M. *Marriage As a Search for Healing* (New York: Brunner/ Mazel, 1997).

Lindenfield, Gael. *Managing Anger* (London: Harper Collins: London, 1993).

Mace, David and Vera. *Love and Anger in Marriage* (England: Pickering Paperbacks, 1982).

Mackay, Hugh. *Why Don't People Listen?* (Australia: Pan MacMillan Publishers, 1994).

Mackay, Hugh. *Generations* (Australia: Pan MacMillan Publishers, 1997).

Malone, Thomas and Patrick. *The Art of Intimacy* (New York: Prentice Hall Press, 1987).

Markman, Howard, Scott Stanley, and Susan Blumberg. *Fighting for Your Marriage* (San Francisco, Calif.: Jossey-Bass Publishing, 1994).

Maslin, Bonnie. *The Angry Marriage* (New York: Hyperion, 1994).

Masters, William H., Virginia Johnson, and Robert Kolodny. *Heterosexuality* (New York: Harper Collins Publishers, 1974).

Minirth, Frank, Brian Newman, and Robert Hemfelt. *Passages of Marriage* (Nashville, Tenn.: Thomas Nelson Publishers, 1991).

Nichols, Michael P. *The Lost Art of Listening* (New York: Guilford Press, 1995).

Noller, Patricia. *Nonverbal Communication and Marital Interaction* (Oxford, England, 1984).

Pearsall, Paul. *A Healing Intimacy* (New York: Crown Trade Paperbacks, 1994).

Penner, Clifford and Joyce. *Men and Sex* (Nashville, Tenn.: Thomas Nelson Publishers, 1997).

Phelps, Stanlee and Nancy Austin. *The Assertive Woman* (California: Impact Publishers, 1975).

Potter-Efron, Ron and Pat. *Letting Go of Anger* (California: New Harbinger Pub. Inc., 1995).

Prager, Karen J. *The Psychology of Intimacy* (New York: Guilford Press, 1995).

Schnarch, David. *Passionate Marriage.* W.W. Norton & Co: NY, 1997.

Simpson, Jeffry A. and Steven Rholes. *Attachment Theory and Close Relationship* (New York: Guilford Press, 1998).

Sperling, Michael B. and William Berman, eds. *Attachment in Adults* (New York: Guilford Press, 1994).

Sternberg, Robert J. and Michael Barnes, eds. *The Psychology of Love* (New Haven, Conn.: Yale University Press, 1988).

Tanenbaum, Joe. *Male and Female Realities* (USA: Tanenbaum Associates, 1992).

Tannen, Deborah. *You Just Don't Understand* (Australia: Random House, 1990).

Tavris, Carol. *Anger: The Misunderstood Emotion* (New York: Simon & Schuster, 1989).

Wallestein, Judith S. and Sandra Blakeslee. *The Good Marriage* (Boston, Mass.: Houghton Mifflin Company, 1995).

Walters, Richard P. *Anger: What to Do About It* (England: Inter-varsity Press, 1981).

Weeks, Dudley. *The Eight Essential Steps to Conflict Resolution* (New York: Penquin Putnam, Inc.,

Wegscheider-Cruse, Sharon. *Coupleship: How to Build a Relationship* (Florida: Health Communications, Inc., 1988).

Wolcott, Ilene,. and Judy Hughes. *Toward Understanding the Reasons for Divorce* (Melbourne: Australian Institute of Family Studies: Working Paper No. 20, 1999).

Yapko, Michael D. *Breaking the Patterns of Depression* (New York: Doubleday, 1997).

Yapko, Michael D. *Hand-Me-Down Blues* (New York: Golden Books, 1999).